Praise for *La Americana*
Selected amongst *Bustle*'s Best Nonfiction Books 2016

"Melanie Bowden Simón recounts her real-life love story in *La Americana*. This is no cut-and-dry romance, though; her memoir tells how she fell in love while on vacation abroad and explores the obstacles she and her now-husband overcame to make their cross-cultural relationship work. Castro's Cuba serves as a particularly interesting backdrop."

—*Bustle*

"WOW! Luis and Melanie will steal your heart!"

—*Fresh Fiction*

"Melanie Bowden Simón took 10 years to be able to write this valentine to her mother and her husband but for the reader it was worth the wait."

—*Global Atlanta*

"Her memoir about her mother, travels to Cuba, and falling in love with her husband, Luís, is moving and gorgeous, and is especially notable for the way in which she portrays Cuba in all its complexity."
—Julie Schwietert Collazo, award-winning journalist and
co-author of the international bestseller,
Pope Francis in His Own Words

"This summer reading list offers up the best new books of summer 2016. . . . A vacation turns into a love story in Melanie Bowden Simón's *La Americana*. The memoir follows as she meets her future husband in Cuba and contends with subsequent relation-

ship obstacles. Her emotional journey also involves dealing with her mother's death and adapting to a new culture."

—*Romper*

"I'm completely captivated by the real-life tale of her cross-cultural romance and thrilling adventures in Castro's Cuba."

—SuthinGirl

"When Simón writes about how in her twenties she decided to comfort herself with foreign travel following the death of her mother, she reminds us that such a trip can mark either the end or the beginning of a personal era, and is a universal experience. In her case, it is both, since it was during her preembargo-lifting vacation to Cuba that she met and fell in love with the man who would become her husband. Simón describes the paranoia of two single women traveling alone to a communist country, the helplessness spawned by language barriers, the herculean efforts to overcome what seemed to be a bottomless bureaucratic quagmire, and, more happily, how she fell in love. Thanks to the recently relaxed relationship between the U.S. and Cuba, Simón's harrowing experiences will stand in contrast to future journeys to our island neighbor."

—*Booklist*

"This is a Prince Charming story; the action peaks with the author's wedding at the beautiful Hotel Nacional in Havana . . . A marriage plot come to life that also incorporates elements of armchair travel."

—*Library Journal*

LA AMERICANA

A MEMOIR

MELANIE BOWDEN SIMÓN

Skyhorse Publishing

Skyhorse Publishing books may be purchased in bulk at special discounts for sales promotion, corporate gifts, fund-raising, or educational purposes. Special editions can also be created to specifications. For details, contact the Special Sales Department, Skyhorse Publishing, 307 West 36th Street, 11th Floor, New York, NY 10018 or info@skyhorse-publishing.com.

Skyhorse® and Skyhorse Publishing® are registered trademarks of Skyhorse Publishing, Inc.®, a Delaware corporation.

Visit our website at www.skyhorsepublishing.com.

10 9 8 7 6 5 4 3 2 1

Library of Congress Cataloging-in-Publication Data is available on file.

Cover design by Laura Klynstra
Cover Photo: iStock

Print ISBN: 978-1-5107-2653-6
Ebook ISBN: 978-1-5107-0256-1

Printed in the United States of America

For Luis and my mom, Martha Parrish McGonigle

Contents

Author's Note/Acknowledgments

I am beyond grateful to my family, who has surrounded me with so much love, support, and encouragement always. First and foremost, this includes my dad, Becky, and my brother, Walter, but also all of the Bowden, Pressly, Wylly, Keightley, Spiller, Yingling, Kelly, and McGonigle clans. My mother-in-law, Ana, my sister-in-law, Anabel, and the many other members of my Cuban family have also welcomed and supported me tremendously from the moment I walked into their lives.

I wouldn't have a book without my agent and friend, Janice Shay, who took a chance on me, an unknown writer, as did my editor, Julie Ganz, at Skyhorse Publishing. I am profoundly appreciative of their efforts.

Neil Young, Ricardo DeSoto, Ashley Bowden, and Chia Chong read early versions of my manuscript and offered not only valuable feedback, but encouragement, for which I am so grateful. Initial edits by Polly Powers Stramm helped me whip my manuscript into enough shape to sell it.

My friends—Allison Wilbur Raddock, Susan Main, and Jacqueline Ballantine—are rock stars, unwavering in their support throughout various stages of my life. And of course, Cynthia Sweet, who made that all-important trip to Cuba with me. To my friends at *Talk* magazine, you made lasting impressions, probably far more than you'll ever know. And a big shout-out to the DeSoto,

Jimenez, and Cruz families, Melissa Owens, Brittany Zimmerman, my colleagues at Armstrong State University, and Savannah's superstar creative set, who inspire and encourage me daily.

Finally, I want to thank Luis and our beautiful children, Ana, Marcos, and Luisito, who give me more joy in life than I ever thought was possible.

Note: Some names have been changed to protect individuals in Cuba.

Chapter 1

Havana

It was April 2001 when our plane touched down in Havana. Cynthia and I stepped off the plane and into crazy humidity, even by my native Georgian standards. On the concrete, military guards in green directed us to glass doors a few feet away, and I crossed the threshold into a frigid blast of air.

My nerves were hopping, and the female passport inspector at the bank-teller-like window didn't help matters. Her steely stare and thick mustache bullied my freckly face, blond hair, and hazel eyes. It was as if the monster under my childhood bed had actually come out and was staring me in the face.

She looked at the photo, at me, at the photo, and at me again. She nodded and I heard a buzz. I looked back at Cynthia and discreetly signaled with one of my thumbs that I was a go. I turned to push through the skinny, wooden door.

Cynthia followed my lead, and soon enough we were outside, where it was complete pandemonium, with hundreds of people lining the gate. Mothers, aunts, and sisters gasped and wept, spotting family members and friends. We pushed our way through the locals only to be bombarded by taxi drivers offering their services. We repeatedly shook our heads no.

While in Cancun, we had spoken to a travel agent who arranged a car service from a Havana hotel to meet us. Through the blur of bodies, we found our guy holding a sign with a jumbled version of my name—MEIYANI BOWDOIN.

Cyn and I slid into the backseat of the black Mercedes and looked out of our respective windows. Our driver was animated and funny, gesticulating wildly, but I couldn't understand him. Cynthia could because she had lived in various Spanish-speaking countries. I met her during my last semester of college while studying abroad in Spain.

It had been three years since I had spent time in Madrid, completing a language minor from the University of Georgia. Yet, had it been English that day, I still couldn't have talked. Mom was gone and sometimes I found it hard just to breathe. So I wrote. Vigorously.

On the way to Hotel Capri, which is located in a residential neighborhood of Havana called Vedado, we saw tank-like 1950s-era Fords and Chevrolets plowing past small, rusted, slightly more modern cars. At bus stops, passengers piled into the strangest breed of vehicle I had ever seen. The base resembled a San Francisco streetcar attached to the front of an eighteen-wheeler truck. An oversize accordion bridged a second section of the bus to give it *Alice in Wonderland* proportions. People held on to overhead rings as heavy diesel fumes created a low, gray skyline. Dilapidated buildings in various states lined the small highway. Chickens and cattle went about their business in overgrown weeds. Suddenly, billboards came at us in three-dimensional proportions.

VIVA LA REVOLUCIÓN! LONG LIVE THE REVOLUTION! FORTY-TWO YEARS OF THE REVOLUTION! WE TRIUMPH WITH SOCIALISM! the signs, scattered throughout the city, screamed in bold yellow and red letters.

Images of Che Guevara, Cuba's socialist revolutionary, decorated the city's concrete with his face on the fronts of buildings, signs, schools, and banners. Even more notably I found myself journaling about a place with no Coca-Cola, no McDonald's, and no Starbucks. In fact, there weren't even any advertisements of any kind there, other than the propaganda.

Arriving at the hotel, we checked in to a room with feeble twin beds that looked as if they came from my grandmother's attic. The low-to-the-ground mattresses caved in when we plopped down on them. A faded, off-white vanity was positioned in the middle of the room and large windows with open curtains gave us a magnificent ocean view.

We packed day bags, headed for the door, and walked the short distance to the Malecón, the city's seawall that borders roughly five miles of Havana's coastline. Gingerly, we maneuvered along the sidewalk's concrete pits and falls as whipping air gusts pushed us around like two grown Raggedy Anns. I half stumbled when a '50s clunker whooshed by, the driver furiously blowing the horn.

"*Hola rubias!*" he belted at us, the two blondies. Cyn and I laughed out loud, but quickly snapped our openmouthed grins shut with the onslaught of thick, black car fumes. The Cuban disappeared around the curb with one last emphatic shout-out. "*Americanaaaaaas!*"

Siphoning diesel from my nostrils with rapid, Lamaze-style breaths, I shared a chuckle, and then a howl, with Cyn as we were simultaneously flipped around by another wicked ocean bluster. No use in fighting, we took its lead, heading back toward our hotel on the corner of Twenty-first and N. We landed facing Hotel Nacional, a Cuban landmark that is known for former guests like Al Capone, Lucky Luciano, Ava Gardner, Frank Sinatra, and their mafia cohorts who rented out entire floors of both Nacional and Capri, where we were staying. Lining the hotel's corridors are photos of diplomats, royals, and celebrities who continue to go there today.

Yet, what caught our attention at that particular moment was a single Cocotaxi, which resembles a large, yellow PAC-MAN. An American man on our flight over suggested that we look for the inexpensive and quick ride as a great way to get around Old Havana. We jumped into the back of one, and speaking Spanish for the first time, I asked to go to Havana Vieja.

The driver, whom I hadn't given any consideration, turned back to us. Almond-shaped caramel eyes, topped with long butterfly-wing lashes, landed directly on mine. It was an intense, swift heart jump that struck me hard. My whole body tensed in self-defense.

Chapter 2

Manhattan and Tina Brown's *Talk*

He introduced himself as Luis and when he did, I thought of my mother. Had she sent this beautiful young man to watch over us?

My mother, whose story was classic in many ways, grew up in Tampa, Florida, in a middle-class home where education was emphasized. My grandfather Jim, a Gregory Peck baritone who wore large, round glasses perched high over a fair-skinned, Germanic jawline and chiseled cheeks, was a professor and chair of English at the University of South Florida. On his crown was a clean swipe, not an angstrom of hair, and the brimmed hats that hung on the front parlor wooden hat rack were sacred for Saturday morning tennis match coverage. My younger brother, Walter, and I called him Grandy and his Gin Rummy game was legendary. Following chocolate-chip-pancake-and-leftover-London-broil breakfasts during scorching summer visits, he schooled us on ten-card draws, runs, and sequences. Taking turns, we parked at a card table with folding chairs set in the living room, and his deep laugh boomed throughout the house, which smelled of an early-morning Folgers brew, if either of us undermined his game. In his presence, my mom, the eldest of his two girls, was relaxed. They shared a love of language and college football and relished in spirited rivalry. Mom, a die-hard Florida Gators fan, propped her arms in a wide V and in her best reptilian impression, pretended to chomp us from her seat on the sofa while Grandy, an Alabama native, vowed imminent defeat at the hands of his beloved Auburn Tigers.

From the kitchen, my grandmother, Lorraine, or Grandmomma as we called her, entertained a world of her own. Her lone voice roiled on low like a late-night TV rerun as the faucet ran long after she'd finished washing dishes. With pre-surgery precision, she scrubbed each of her long, slender fingers, pressing along the dorsal veins and then over the top arteries before moving to the blue, spidery arches of her hands. The ceremonial drying towel morphed into a dishrag that gave one last countertop sweep before retiring it to the laundry bin in the garage.

Standing at the crux of the kitchen and dining room, Grandmomma, a slim-figured former basketball star with cropped, loose white curls, peppered us with light questions about school, sports, and our friends while the sharp glare of plastic, snuggly fit over the living room sofa and chairs, cut through the doorway behind her.

Sometimes when Grandmomma laughed, she blinked furiously in a maladjusted camera shutter sort of twitch while pinching the side hinge of her oversize eyeglass frames to boost a nose slip. To us, it was a benign gesture, but to my mom it signaled anger. Mom's impression was dead on, but it only surfaced during rare recounts of her childhood memories.

At Chamberlain High School, my mom was Marti, an easygoing, popular, and pretty blonde who made mostly As and won spelling bees. But at home she was Martha and under the watchful eye of my grandmother, too skinny. She could have been smarter if she studied more.

6

Mom found refuge in Grandy's library, tucked into the far back corner of their home. The rows of literature, both classic and modern, sat next to the great playwrights and they whispered to her in clear and vibrant tones. She responded in the only way she could—as a teenager, she became an active theater member, playing out their roles as often as possible. She also was a good writer and for years talked about drafting a novel. While an English major at the University of Florida, my mom met my father, Walter, an attractive, honorable young man studying business. He and my mom dated throughout college and married just before he was called to serve in Vietnam. On her own, Mom briefly returned home with her parents and taught high school English. Following my dad's return a year later, she worked various lightweight secretary jobs, though I'm certain she secretly dreamed of a creative life—eccentricities included—in New York City.

Yet, life being what it was, and considering the roles for women at that time, my mom settled into married life. Not that it was bad. She was married to a nice and caring man whose focus was his family. Later, I was born and Walter came two and a half years later.

My mom, Martha Parrish, 1969 (*courtesy of Melanie Simón*).

However, in time she and my father had little left in common; while she loved us, she sought personal inspiration in local theaters. My father worked vigorously in banking, seeking solace in his children and nature in any free time he could muster. They divorced when I was ten. My father remarried Becky, who became a very important person in my life, a second mother. Mom and I eventually moved to Atlanta, which was a pit stop on her way to the bright and alluring lights of New York. When I graduated from high school, she made her last leap. After a year of freelance PR jobs in the city, she landed a full-time one with David Mamet's nonprofit organization, the TADA! Youth Theater on the Lower West Side of Manhattan. Perks included preview theater tickets, which she gobbled up. Routinely, she shared invites with me, her evergreen baby girl who visited during college and later when I settled into New York in 1999.

I loved every second, sitting in the darkened, iconic settings on and off-Broadway with my mom. She introduced me to the subtle and dry wit of Tony winners Frank Wood and Edie Falco in *Side Man*; the dysfunctional, mad genius of John Leguizamo in *Spic-O-Rama*; and the prim, fluid voices of Patti Lupone, Audra McDonald, and Brian Stokes Mitchell that burrowed and popped under my skin. I erupted at the Ambassador Theater on West Forty-ninth when Savion Glover invited audience members to the toe-tapped wooden side stage during "Bring in 'da Noise, Bring in 'da Funk." Our legs crunched in early-twentieth-century architecture, I leaped over my mom and neighboring patrons in a clumsy dash to the stage where I planted myself directly behind Savion, who stopped time with his raw, poetic, and powerhouse foot thrusts and heel slaps. I'm not a tapper, but I had to be there, to be a part of that energy, and I carried the nearly religious experience back to the tiny seat row where my mom waited for me, wearing the same wild look of joy on her face. It was clear then that as a young adult, I had become her extension, playing out inspired bursts that she had learned to cap in her childhood home.

High off the performances, we always shared dinner, offering praise or potshots. With one hand bridged along the side of her face, Mom held a chardonnay stem with the other and twinkled in a post-theater glow.

A few years later when she scored the PR director position for the Yale School of Drama and its professional in-house group, the Yale Repertory Theatre, it was a high mark. She was able to promote visiting alumni like Meryl Streep and Sigourney Weaver, as well as bold and temperamental playwrights like John Guare, who directed Laura Linney in *Landscape of the Body*.

While there she married Jim McGonigle, a whip-smart and kind man seventeen years her senior, after a meet-up at the Lambs Club in Manhattan. Age apart, they complemented each other well with a love of solid performances, travel, and mild smart-ass satire. She was the calm to his feisty and after her early retirement from Yale, they shuttled back and forth between their Morristown, New Jersey, home and Manhattan apartment. So when I moved to New York in March 1999 as a newbie University of Georgia graduate, to my delight, this meant that I was back within close proximity to Mom. With fresh journalism and Spanish degrees in hand, I had packed my Honda Civic with a mix of hand-me-down bedsheets, lamps, and side tables, as well as the heaviest clothes from my closet. I knew nights would still be cold once I crossed the Virginia line.

On the front seat of my car sat an overstuffed, padded manila envelope. Inside were a handful of articles I had written for professors and the local paper in Athens, Georgia. It had been my first real job—writing about town happenings. I also brought along a thesis paper following the career of Tina Brown, who once headed *The New Yorker* and *Vanity Fair*.

So, a year later after various temp jobs, when the head of a Manhattan entertainment staffing agency asked me if I knew who Tina

Brown was and would I like to sit in as her second assistant at *Talk* magazine, I thought he was joking. He wasn't.

I sweated three interviews for a job that wasn't even permanent. The first two rounds were with managing editors, and finally I qualified to meet with Margaret, Tina's first assistant. In time, Margaret—or Mags as I now call her—became my dear friend, but at first she completely intimidated me. She is only slightly older than I was, but she was so very serious that it threw me. I had never met anyone my age so put together. Yet, behind the suit and her small, oval glasses, I sensed that she was fair.

Fair she was. I started at *Talk* a few days later, knowing that, because of the stress level, a string of girls already had come and gone from the same job. I was innocent in a small-town kind of way and sat in a chair tucked in the far corner of the building, taking on any number of tasks that Margaret delegated to me. She briefed me on this, on that. Do this, try not to do that. And always—always—pick up the phone.

I remember being horribly nervous when someone once asked me to take a Diet Coke to Tina in the middle of a meeting. She was with a group of Miramax execs, and I became nauseous at the thought of interrupting. Did Tina like ice? Would she want a straw? Would anyone even look at me?

A couple of the girls ribbed me: Tina only likes one cube of ice and the straw cocked to the right side, not the left. NOT THE LEFT. Gallantly, I took the bait: I dropped one cube of ice in, but I couldn't get the damn straw to stay on the right side. Finally, the girls caved in a fit of laughter, and caught in my own absurdity, I did too.

It didn't take long to realize that Tina didn't care much about ice or straws. She had better things to think about. In its infancy *Talk* was a powerful magazine. Staff members frequently turned up in New York's gossip columns or as inserts in other magazines for being fabulous, rich, and influential. Tina was known for throwing powerhouse parties, which were impressive to even the most impressive.

I tried to take it all in stride, but when I helped set up an intimate dinner at her Manhattan home, with place cards that read BILL CLINTON, ROBERT DeNIRO, and BARBRA STREISAND—among thirty or so others—it was hard for my heart not to skip a beat.

Yet it was my mother's excitement that spilled, as she became near giddy when I gave any insight, insipid or not, about our goings-on at work. In reality, her joy came from watching me chase my dreams—something she didn't do at my age. When I was hired permanently as an assistant to Joe Armstrong, a vice president who crossed both the magazine and book divisions, my mom began to call me on my direct line routinely, enthusiastically, to make sure I had seen the most current gossipy bit on *Talk* or Tina. What she didn't know was that if anyone in our office sneezed, it would be reported. Reported—it would be seized, scrutinized, stored, and rocketed to our office. The universe did not permit *Talk* media to go unnoticed.

Her calls were brief and funny. This was her way of touching base with me in a nonintrusive way. However, one afternoon she called with news of her own. I was slammed at work, funneling one effort into the other. My job had become as physical as mental; I was up and down constantly, all but running a race to keep things moving as needed.

Still, when Mom's call came in, I picked up.

"Hey," I said. "I'm kind of crazy, but what's up?"

"Well"—and she paused slightly—"I went to the doctor today."

She had been feeling unusually tired and nauseous in the late afternoons, promptly at the five o'clock mark. I stopped multitasking and put down both the pen in my right hand and the papers in my left. I grabbed the receiver wedged into the crook of my neck.

"OK. Are you OK?"

"He found some unusual cells. They're cancerous," she said.

Chapter 3

Gringas in Castro's Cuba

I wished Mom could have been with me when I met Luis. He was strikingly handsome. In crisp blue jeans and a neatly pressed Havana Club T-shirt, he was elegant in every way—his bone structure, the way he sat, his jet-black hair shining in the sunlight.

With his nod, his sky-reaching lashes flickered twice in a Morse code yes to our Havana Vieja trip request and turned left to align us again with the Malecón. He must have a huge ego, I thought. Way too pretty.

I reset my sights and tried to take in the slideshow as we moved briskly next to the ocean. The late-afternoon sun cast a heavy shadow over the buildings. Life bustled inside those walls and across balconies where clotheslines were strung, but I couldn't figure how anyone could live in something that looked like it might collapse at any moment.

With their interiors on display, each piece of architecture is distinct. Many of the buildings are centuries old, ornate in their Spanish, French, and Greek rounds, curves, and columns. Other buildings are more modern, Art Deco I'd read, and most unfortunately, a handful salute the former USSR and its brief, but powerful 1980s reign in Cuba. The concrete block buildings looked ridiculously rude standing near the European beauties.

In cultural overload I couldn't absorb too many details, but as we moved quickly along the perimeter, the broad landscapes of pinks, greens, blues, and yellows reached inside me. Chills ran down my arms despite the ninety-degree temperature. The entire city looked as if it had been dipped into the ocean and pulled back up to dry with its colors faded and dripping.

As I glanced to my left, a large rock formation appeared. Perhaps a tower was affixed to it, jetting over the sea. My eyes flashed down for a nanosecond, catching our driver's eyes in the rearview mirror as he changed lanes. He looked back at me. As we neared the rock, my attention shot back to it, more fortress-like in its silhouette. Again, my eyes jumped to the side and I caught a glimpse of Luis's hands. Smallish and square, they were clean and masculine in their grip of the taxi's black handlebars. A white-faced Swatch with a silver and gold band circled his wrist precisely, as if Italian-tailored. In a minimal and exact language of its own, Luis's span of gestures spoke within a tight body circumference. His legs stretched in direct line with the clutch and gas pedals, never once splaying, as his elbows tucked tightly into his sides. Slight head turns were the sole signals that we were about to curve in a new direction on Havana's streets. And the only visible hint of stress detected in his otherwise confident structure peeped from his pink nails, which were bitten to the core.

With force, I pushed my eyes back to the rock.

"What is that?" I asked in Spanish.

"You don't know Cuba?" he said as he turned his head back to look at me. His Spanish was fast, but the comment was short so I got it.

I shook my head no.

With that, he crawled out of his clamshell and began to tell us about his city.

What I was looking at was El Morro—a fort built by the Spanish in the sixteenth and seventeenth centuries when Havana's harbor was attacked repeatedly by pirates. I stretched as far back to history class as I could: In 1492 Christopher Columbus sailed the ocean blue. I remembered vague facts about Hispaniola, but not much about Cuba. I don't think we ever learned more than Kennedy's Bay of Pigs disaster in the '60s.

In Spanish-speaking countries, Columbus is referred to as Cristóbal Colón. He described Cuba as the "loveliest land ever beheld by human eyes." Riding the country's edge, it was easy to understand why.

For transporting riches, Havana became a key stop between the new and old worlds. As a result, Havana was the most protected city in the Americas at that time. I had to read more later about the country's history and assume as much, because I didn't get it the first go-round. Luis's words were diluted by my inability to concentrate. I wanted to understand, but it was still too much work for me. Instead I fell into a trance of sorts, taken in by the ocean's power. We eventually slowed to a stop in Plaza de Armas in Havana Vieja.

Luis turned off the taxi and posed a question that I didn't understand. Cynthia explained that he could come back later and give us a tour of Havana. He turned so we could talk in private. I jabbed Cyn with my elbow and widened my eyes. She laughed and told him, "Yes, please come back in an hour and a half."

"*Adios, Luis,*" we said in unison with a wave as we lowered ourselves onto the cobblestone walk.

We moved on and crawled through an outdoor market that didn't sell much more than plastic busts of Fidel Castro and Che, straw hats, and crocheted bikinis made for either ten-year-old girls or flagrant exhibitionists. Cyn and I redirected and navigated toward Havana's side streets, large stones underfoot. We wanted to see, smell, and attempt to feel how locals lived, not how they peddled the same goods month in and month out.

People were everywhere, sitting on the street and spilling from their front parlors. They laughed and talked with their hands as much as their mouths, but I quickly picked up on a uniform look of boredom. I had that same look the summer I spent collecting money at my post on Martha's Vineyard where only a few visitors paid to cross the path to Chappaquiddick Beach. Many wanted to know if this was where Senator Kennedy had had his ill-fated night with Mary Jo. It was. They walked on and I remained in place, unimaginably bored.

In my hometown of Savannah, residential doors typically stay closed, opened only by invitation, like most of the US. Yet, in the narrow streets of Havana, front doors and windows, with their decorative birdcage bars, were sprawled open, all but begging us to take a peek. There was no way around it: we were Curious Georges, leaving textbook chapters on communism and the Cuban Missile Crisis to American classrooms.

Broken granite and tile floors were swept clean and topped with rocking chairs, oversize religious figures, and makeshift altars covered in what looked like beads, coins, and tapas-sized sweets. We heard blazing televisions, laughter, and the blended Spanish and African rhythms I love—salsa, son, and rumba. Together the sounds formed a paste, an actual texture in the air, which I instinctively sensed bound together more than just notes.

Its essence registered in me, in the middle of all of that chaotic energy, and I was reminded of many New York nights, burrowed in crowded blues bars with my eyes closed, head swaying on beat.

Like the music of Cuba, blues tells tales of oppression and inequality, tucked behind soulful riffs and a heavy dose of humor.

It was after several blocks, speaking broken Spanish to locals, avoiding those that called out, "Hey, *rubias* (blondes)," or, "You, lady, you want be my friend?" that I fully appreciated the power of the music. It cupped my wobbly soul, and in turn, every ounce of me responded. My feet shuffled in constant motion, in small salsa swirls, pushing my hips to follow suit. On the street, in corner shops where we looked at postcards or in packed bars where we drank mojitos and Cuba Libres (this drink translates to Free Cuba, but what and who is free in Cuba, I wondered for a fleeting moment). Usually groups of three or four musicians and one singer in some variance moved me so much that I forgot where I was or who I was. The music possessed me and I welcomed it. It felt good to feel good.

Men sat in chairs on street corners, refueling cigarette lighters with spray cans of propane gas. At home they would have thrown the used lighters away. Tourists and Cubans covered the streets while great automobile giants pushed through. *VROOOOM, VROOOOM!* The drivers floored the gas pedals in an attempt to clear the roads. The exaggerated masculinity gave the impression of flexed muscles in motion.

Up close I could see that some of the car doors were clinging for their very lives. Flattened Coke cans were wedged in one; others were jacked up with tightly wound string or chicken wire. Coming to life in front of me were Cuba's clichés—car windows down, raging good salsa, weeping boleros, and fat cigars hanging from thick fingers, trailing smoke behind them unapologetically.

Patrolling the downtown blocks were well-armed and stone-faced policemen, meant to insure safety, but mostly, they made me feel uncomfortable. In their presence, the catcalls subsided, but the vast amount of militia was unnerving, as if Castro himself were watching my every move. After some time I realized that the guards were focused on their citizens, whom they watched and approached in uneasy closeness.

The sense of adventure I felt walking those streets was distinct. I've always thrived on new energy, foreign languages, smells, and sounds, but there the sensations that passed through me were overwhelmingly powerful.

I'll say it—it was exhilarating to be somewhere I wasn't supposed to be. I'm not a hard rebel, but it was a little like sneaking a drink from your mom's liquor cabinet at thirteen or getting into a bar with a fake ID for the first time at seventeen.

What I wasn't prepared for was the reality forming in front of me. The Cuban essence, so obviously based in pleasure, apparent in even the little bit I had seen, suppressed by such control, was scary. The paranoia was something I felt, though I didn't understand, and it managed to creep into my system upon my arrival. The contrast of my curiosity, happiness to just be there, and newfound fear left me both intrigued and on edge.

Cynthia's healthy sense of direction eventually got us back to Point A after we wandered in what I thought was freestyle aimlessness. Had I been leading, we would have spent hours circling the beautiful cathedral in the Spanish-style square, situated in the middle of Old Havana.

As we walked up, we spotted Luis sitting in his Cocotaxi, number 92, talking to another driver parked next to him. He was on time, which, from what I had read about Cuban culture, was a novelty.

He looked at me and said, "*Hola.*"

"*Hola,*" I returned meekly and jumped in the backseat without looking him in the eye. I flushed, embarrassed, though I didn't know why.

As soon as we took off, he and Cynthia started talking. I didn't listen or try to decipher their conversation. It was overdrive for my brain and I was content to just feel.

We swung in and around different neighborhoods: more into Old Havana, then Miramar and its Fifth Avenue, which used to hold the same reverence as its distant Manhattan cousin. The blocks were the picture of aged elegance, lined with mansions and a closed country club that I imagined once entertained American Coca-Cola and Ford execs. Like all businesses and private property, the buildings were rendered to the state in 1959 once Castro took office. Today they are home to foreign consulates and embassies, as well as government offices. Next we drove into a large plaza with a monolithic silhouette of Che on a concrete building. Though he represents peace around the world, the sheer size of his portrait loomed most unsettlingly. *We're watching you* is all I felt. Maybe I had read too much. Maybe I needed to relax, not feed into the American hype.

As Luis spoke, we turned to another monument for José Martí. The prolific intellectual, poet, and war hero died in 1895, defending Cuba in the War of Independence against Spain. His image can be seen throughout the country on a smattering of billboards and painted walls. Cuba's deities were among us. Their power was distinct and so was my smallness.

Eventually we made it back to Vedado, our hotel's neighborhood, where Luis told us that he and his family had lived for many years (as noted by Cynthia who was translating about 90 percent of this to me). My interest in Luis and his family piqued slightly as we glided in front of his former house, a mansion with an enormous front patio and well-attended garden. Hot pink bougainvillea ran wildly over the stoop and was astoundingly beautiful in its disarray. The building itself was aged, but not abandoned. I caught something Luis said about running a B&B there. Tourists from all over stayed and loved his mom's food.

He said that they had lived there until recently, but had had to move. I might have asked questions, but the US government's website on Cuba had left me sufficiently paranoid about the country's communist ways and many travel books warned of talking about any and all things political to locals. I assumed it was best to stay quiet.

Luis pulled up to the hotel's stoop. He and Cynthia talked about meeting up that night to go out. She was very clear—we wanted to go where locals went to dance. *Gringas* (white American girls) we were, but we wanted to shake it *con Cubanos.*

Chapter 4

Tick Tock

July 2000

When Mom told me about the cancer, I went mute. It was as if someone had slapped my mouth shut. The room started to spin and anyone who passed was a blurry vision.

She told me that there was nothing to worry about. She might possibly have to do a little chemotherapy over the summer, but that would put the infantile cells out of their misery.

"OK," I said. I didn't know how to respond. I was out of sorts, but chose to believe what she said.

I hung up and not minutes later my boss, Joe Armstrong, walked in.

"Mellll!" he called to me. Joe is from Texas and his way is fun.

"Hi," I responded, trying to put on a normal face.

"Mel, can you put this in the mail for me, please?"

"Sure," I said as I took the bill and envelope from him. I stuffed it in with the accompanying check and pulled a stamp out from the drawer. I sealed it shut and put it on my desk.

"Mel," Joe said as he picked up the envelope. "Hon, the bill is turned around. The mailman won't know where to deliver it."

He said it nicely, but I felt stupid. *He's going to fire me,* I thought.

"That won't work, will it?" I said, forcing a meek laugh and I took it back. "Sorry. That won't happen again."

"Mel," he said, looking into me. "Are you OK?"

"Yes, yes, I'm fine. Just a lot going on!" It was fake, that last exclamation I made, but I didn't want him to feel like I couldn't do my job. I also didn't feel like answering questions about something I didn't understand.

A week later, I kept looking at the clock while Mom underwent tests at Sloan Kettering Hospital, one of the greatest cancer hospitals in the world. She was supposed to call me around noon.

By four o'clock and still no word from her, I was nervous. I started leaving messages at her apartment. Finally, she called, upbeat, revealing no signs of stress.

"Well," she said, "they want to keep me overnight. My calcium levels are a little high. It's no big deal. They'll just put me on a drip."

I didn't know what that meant, but her composure calmed mine. My imagination didn't run free; though scared, I remained positive. I was able to get back to work without too much distraction. At the end of my workday, I called her room to see if she wanted mindless magazines or something to bide her time in the hospital. My stepfather, Jim, picked up the phone.

"Hello." His voice was heavy. Instinctively, it frightened me.

"Is Mom there?" I asked.

"Yes."

I waited for him to say more, but he didn't.

"Can I speak to her?"

"I think you need to get over here right away."

My stomach ripped to my throat. "What's wrong?"

"Just get over here." He hung up.

I threw down the phone, shaking, and grabbed my purse. I left my computer on and papers piled on my desk. I hurried to the elevator and realized I needed money for the cab ride to the hospital. Chase Bank, at the other end of the long block, seemed far away. But as I bolted out the front door of the building, I reached the opposite corner in record time. The otherwise clean sidewalk was littered with bank receipts and I scrambled for my debit card, which was the only way to gain access to the door. Where is it? Where is it? Shit, shit, shit. I fumbled. I couldn't find it, buried in my mess of a bag. Got it. I slid it in the slot and circled around to the first empty machine.

My mind was racing. I had to force myself to focus on the computer screen in front of me. Negative. My freaking bank account was negative twenty-three dollars. I was single in the city with magazine assistant pay and at that time I was not known for handling money well to begin with. My father, who was not only a bank CEO back then but was probably counting pennies in the womb, may have been disappointed, but not surprised.

Still, he would have said, "Mel? How much do you need to get you through to the next paycheck?"

In my independent state, I would have said I'd be fine and not to worry about it. And he would have quietly deposited a couple hundred dollars into my account. He has always taken care of me in his solid, discreet way.

Unable to call him (without a cell phone at the time—imagine that!), I ran back up to the office. Margaret. Where is she? I looked up and down the halls until I saw her in the middle of a roundabout gossip section in one of the associate editors' offices during one of her rare breaks. Visibly out of sorts, I stood outside the cracked door and asked if I could borrow her for a minute.

"Of course," she said and quickly came to my side. "What's wrong, what's wrong, Mellie?" she kept asking me as she followed me down the hall.

I lost it. I started to hyperventilate and couldn't form words. She pulled me into Tina's vacant office, shut the door, and sat in the chair. I was kneeling on the floor, like a child in mid-prayer, my head in her lap, sobbing. I couldn't breathe.

"What is it? What is it?" She was begging me for an answer. "Your job?" I shook my head no. "A guy?" No again. "Are you sick?" No. "Your family?" Yes, this time. "Oh, God, Mellie. What happened?"

I burst out, "My mom. She has cancer."

It was what I hadn't been willing to admit to myself before. She didn't just have cancerous cells, ready to be zapped away in some fantasy game of *Star Wars*. This was a potentially fatal disease. At twenty-four, it was way too much for me to swallow.

I don't even know what Margaret said after that, but I remember that she was petting my hair and crying. I explained my money situation and she said, "Of course, of course," and left for a moment. She returned with fifty dollars in her hand in case I needed to get Mom flowers or magazines or anything else. She always thinks of things like that. I pulled myself together, enough to get on the elevator anyway. I managed to get a cab to the hospital, unaware that it would be a ride that would become all too familiar.

Short of jumping from the moving car, I threw too much money at the driver and ran inside to take the elevator to the twelfth floor. Mom was waiting to get into a private room, but because she needed immediate attention, she shared a room with another woman. A curtain was pulled around the side of the bed and I saw Jim, his eyes bloodshot, sitting in the corner chair. He looked at me with no sense of recognition. I came around the white veil to my mom, who was hooked up to an IV. She looked so small and feeble in that bed.

Her wide eyes met mine. Their vagueness clashed with my intense stare.

"Hi," I said and kissed her on the cheek. "What's going on?" I asked, trying to be patient while dying inside.

"Did you tell her yet?" Jim asked, as if he had just realized I was in the room.

She shook her head no.

He simply got up and walked out.

She reached her hand out and took mine. "It's bad."

Mom became foggy right in front of me when she spoke. She was a dream of some sort, not my mother.

"They've found a large tumor. It's in my liver"—and she started to draw a picture on her torso—"that comes up near my heart." I didn't understand. My mind sharpened. Complete tunnel vision. Details in the room and around her bed turned into simple shapes—squares and circles and a configuration of dots that had no meaning to me, like hieroglyphics.

I had no idea what she was telling me. Children look to their parents for answers, and I was a little girl again, searching for guidance.

Her voice picked up, positive in tone: "They have the best doctors here. They have medical teams looking at my CAT scans."

She explained that there wasn't any real treatment for her type of cancer, which was advanced at that point. As I understood it later, because at that time I couldn't absorb technical information, the doctors told her it was inoperable because the cancer had crawled up her aorta. Surgery would have killed her, as she would lose too much blood in the process.

As I attempted to take in what she was telling me, her voice started to fade, descending into a monotone, like she was rattling off a monologue she used to practice for her beloved theater auditions. That's when she said she had a couple of years left to be with me, my brother, and Jim . . .

. . . a couple of years left. What the fuck was she talking about?

25

Tears were in her eyes when Jim walked back into the room. He sat down in the wooden school chair. I could feel his weight, the weight of the room, the weight of the tumor, the weight of my chest, and the bearing of my mother's sadness.

I said that I didn't understand. She told me that sometimes bad things happen to good people. She didn't know why, but that was outrageously unacceptable to me. We weren't in Bible school. This wasn't some lesson for the day. This was my mother, sick. I couldn't be as carefree and forgiving as that.

The nurses came in. That was my cue to come up for air. I asked Mom if she wanted anything. She told me raspberry sorbet would be nice. *Great*, I thought. *Get me out, get me out.*

Chapter 5

Who's Afraid of Uncle Sam?

Cradled in the low-slung bed in Cuba, I watched as the sun lowered, casting dark shadows across our room as I thought about my mom and our similarities. Beyond our love of the arts and sometimes ridiculous sense of humor, our physical traits were almost one for one. My mouth, nose, eyes, snakelike eyebrows, and cheekbones mimick hers to an almost exact degree, as do many of my gestures.

Her good friend, Leslie, described her as a mix between Marilyn Monroe and Diane Keaton. Highly appropriate, only I favored the Keaton side as a tomboy growing up.

I wanted to sit with her and talk like we used to. My eyes watered. Cynthia spoke and cut my thoughts in half. I squeegeed the excess tears back as far as I could so they wouldn't run over.

"What are we doing here?" she said, looking at me.

I shook my head slightly. "I really have no idea."

We both laughed as I wiped the corners of my eyes with the side of my hand.

Cynthia and I had become good friends in 1998 during our final college semester in Madrid while in the same study abroad program via my undergraduate degree at University of Georgia and hers at a college in Massachusetts. Daytime hours were spent wandering sites like Museo Nacional del Prado and the Royal Palace as I enviously studied her Spanish-speaking abilities, heightened after summers spent in Guatemala and Belize. In the wee early-morning hours we hobbled on high heels to Puerto del Sol, Madrid's central square, and shared Spain's magnificent fried doughnut-like creations, *churros con chocolate*, and coffee after full nights of dancing, red-faced and tipsy from hours of salsa and Spanish rock 'n' roll.

Later, when I was in New York, she visited from Boston and we hit Manhattan's throwback disco ball parties in gold lame and faux fur, but when my mom became sick, Cynthia stayed in especially close touch, calling frequently. She was the first person I reached out to after seeing *Buena Vista Social Club* in that Manhattan movie theater. A solid dancer and lover of all things Latino, I knew she'd be my only friend up for going to Cuba with me. Her Cancun-born boyfriend offered the help of his mother, a travel agent who set us up with visas and hotels. The original trip was set for January 2001 while my mother was ill, but not critical. But when it became evident my mother wouldn't live much beyond the New Year, we held off until May, a full four months after my mom had died.

Travel to Cuba was initially intended as an off-path adventure, but morphed into something far more powerful for me, a motherless girl, by spring. It had become an escape, a desperately needed break from life without Mom and a failed career that was just beginning to take off in New York.

"Do you want to shower first?" Cynthia asked.

"No, you go ahead."

Cyn pulled herself out of bed and I dozed while she bathed.

She emerged with just a sliver of a towel wrapped and tucked around her, and attempted to untangle open-air taxi hair. I left her to it and lifted myself from the sandpit. The bathroom was puny and well-used, but clean.

The water didn't get very hot, but the coolness felt good. Black streams fell from my hair and body. As I stepped out to reach for my handkerchief towel, I looked in the mirror. My face was heavy—not in size, but the weight of internal baggage was clearly evident.

We dressed and headed out to eat. The first place we went lost all power, so we left. The next place didn't have any gas and only served cold fries and some mystery meat. Starving, we took it, handpicking the fries alone.

Luis was going to be at the hotel soon so we hurriedly paid with the American dollar, which had become legal tender next to the Cuban peso in 1993 after the fall of the Soviet Union. During what was called the *Período Especial* or Special Period, Cuba was hit with a devastating economic depression in the early to mid-'90s after the loss of its European backer and was forced to open its doors to tourists and investors from the rest of the world.

The dollar became the primary currency, but technically, via the US embargo, it shouldn't have been. President Clinton largely ignored what was going on in Cuba and President Bush did until 2004, when he lashed out at Swiss banks funneling the cash transactions.

As Americans we weren't allowed to pull money from US-based bank accounts or carry traveler's checks and therefore had to carry an uncomfortable amount of cash on us. I ended up stashing wads in and around body parts for fear of it being stolen from our room.

We scurried back to the hotel's lobby and for the first time, I noticed a series of posters behind glass encasings. One flashed Uncle Sam growling and clawed, across a body of water from a Cuban soldier, a gun in hand, who shouted, "*Señores Imperialistas! No Les Tenemos Absolutamente Ningun Miedo!*"

Loosely translated: Mr. Imperialists: We have absolutely no fear!

I knew it was all propaganda, stemming from Kennedy's mess at the Bay of Pigs, in which 1,200 of the 1,400 Cuban exiles who launched the attack were imprisoned for twenty months. Bobby Kennedy, who was attorney general at the time, did his best to make amends, pleading with American pharmaceutical and baby food manufacturers to make contributions and finally, he was able to do so, loading Castro with fifty-three million dollars worth of goods in exchange for US prisoners.

But President Kennedy took the hit hard and launched Operation Mongoose, a plan to take down Castro's government and the Cuban economy, in retaliation. There were mentions of a possible assassination.

Maybe I should have taken the cartoons personally, as an American in a hotel run by a government in my face, but I knew to let it go. This was pure politics, government to government, and at that time, politics was far from interesting to me.

"There's Luis," Cynthia said, and nodded to the front door.

I turned around and there he was in an immaculately ironed European fit white shirt against his dark brown skin. He picked up the lobby phone and called our room. Like schoolgirls, we giggled and let him dial and then hang up after what must have been a good ten rings.

"Luis," we called together and waved as he turned toward us. He smiled.

We both received a customary kiss on the cheek before following him out. His eyes met mine briefly before I headed out the door to the Cocotaxi without looking at him again.

All of the travel books I'd read before going to Cuba mentioned that tourists should pay for dinner or drinks, or both, for their guides. I had extra cash set aside in my purse, but Luis never asked, and insisted that we didn't pay for him at all. Instead, he sat as we took to the dance floor of a cavernous bar that played salsa and Madonna's "Holiday."

"Whole-eee-day," the Cubans sang out loud.

Salsa re-emerged and Cyn drifted back next to Luis while I jumped into the mix, losing myself next to Cubans who expressed themselves in such fluid waves that I couldn't compare it to anything else I had experienced. Their top halves defied their lower counterparts; the energy was intoxicating.

From left court, in choreographed structure, two young peacocks, tall and treacherously sexy, strutted onto the dance floor across from me, pairing themselves with two older men in the same sort of handcrafted, leather shoes I saw across Spain and our side trip to Italy.

Italians, I guessed, based on their shoes. The men petrified on the spot as the women pressed their long torsos into their backs and laced their hands under their arms and through to their chests. I couldn't put the puzzle together. How could these girls, no more than eighteen or nineteen and genuinely beautiful, crawl on middle-aged, bloated-bellied men?

Luis pointed out that they were prostitutes. I'm always slow to accept those real-life kinds of things.

At some point, Luis had to leave, but said he would send someone to pick us up, if we could give him a time. Promptly at 3:00 a.m., a colleague of his arrived to take us home. That night I slept like the dead. It was the first time I had slept through in one solid stroke—no nightmares, no flashbacks, no fear—in nearly a year, since Mom's diagnosis. Just blackness in all its beauty.

Chapter 6

Maria Victoria
and the *Casa Particular*

The next morning we were ravenous. Soy and granola bars from home filled in the breakfast gap, but we needed a real meal.

In Cynthia's travel book was a listing for a *casa particular*, or private home near our hotel. For about five to ten bucks each, we could have a home-cooked meal.

In Cuba, street signs aren't easy to come by. Instead of clear, eye-level markers, the signs often are monogrammed into corner angles of buildings or on cement triangles, raised only a few inches off the ground. We followed the alphabetized streets until we reached H. As Cynthia noted, it's a city for Cubans, not tourists. But, as we found, Cubans were approachable and gave amicable directions.

At the *casa particular,* we found the doorbell hanging from its hinge and a locked front door. In a few minutes, an older woman with a kind face walked up the small set of stairs into the building. Cynthia asked if we were at Maria Victoria's house.

She smiled, replied yes, and motioned for us to follow her.

We were to go up one flight of stairs and then left until we reached the end of the hallway. We thanked her, ascended a dark, musty spiral stairwell, and both began to laugh hysterically at the lengths to which we were going to find good food. Cynthia took a picture of me for posterity.

On the second floor, there were no numbers on the row of doors. At the last one, Cyn shrugged and knocked. A friendly, cheerful woman greeted us, as though she had been expecting us.

"Is this Maria Victoria's?" asked Cynthia.

"*Si, mi vida*," the woman replied. This literally translates to "Yes, my life," and it's an affectionate way Cubans often speak, as if you are the most important person in their lives. And, on occasion, you just might be.

Cynthia had the address flagged in her travel book, which was tucked under her arm, and she pulled it out to show to the woman, as if to validate why we were standing in her doorway.

"We would like to eat here, if possible," Cynthia said to her in Spanish.

"*Entra, entra,*" said the woman, waving her hands for us to go in. I felt uncertain, but we headed inside anyway.

This was Maria Victoria and we stood in the parlor of her one-level apartment with a balcony overlooking the street. She explained that she would have to go and buy the food and prepare a meal for the following day.

The only jobs available to Cubans at that time were provided by the government, and workers were paid a stipend of 240 Cuban pesos, roughly equivalent to ten US dollars a month, though the cost of living did not match their resources. Doctors, lawyers, and military generals would make the same wages as the woman who hands out toilet paper at the airport bathroom or Luis as our driver and guide.

It has been told to me on many occasions that doctors frequently receive throwbacks—dinner at a patient's house, cash, or a nice bottle of rum—for extra care, as do high-ranking military men, who are the first in line for generous helpings of meat and specialty items that come into the country. Taxi drivers and waiters can make decent money in tips at more popular spots like the Hotel Nacional. Discovering this made me wonder why people even bothered going to school at all, despite the famously good, free education.

All Cuban citizens are given books for food rations, which they then take to the local *bodega* to receive about six pounds of rice, ten ounces of beans, six pounds of sugar—three white and three raw—and ten eggs per person for the month. They also get six ounces of coffee, cigarettes for some adults, a half pound of powdered milk (for children under seven), two pounds of potatoes per person, one bar of soap and one bar of dishwashing soap (when the government feels like it, according to a Cuban friend living in the US), and one tube of toothpaste per family. At times they're also given a quarter of a chicken per person for the month, as well as a quarter pound of vegetable oil and one piece of bread per day for each family member. In addition, they also are allotted a half pound of salt every three months.

This would explain why someone like Maria Victoria, who we learned was an architect, sought visitors like us to eat in her home.

"What would you like tomorrow?" she asked us.

We both preferred seafood to meat. The rest was up to her. She said she would cook fish, beans, rice, and fried plantains if that suited us. The saliva glands in my mouth swelled at the mere mention.

"OK, great. We'll see you tomorrow," Cyn and I overlapped.

Maria Victoria escorted us back to the door. As we crossed into the hallway, she said in the lower regions of her voice, "Don't tell anyone you were here, OK?"

As if the paradox that she was listed in any number of travel guides around the world didn't exist, we nodded and walked down the stairwell.

Chapter 7

Click Clack Go the Tiles

On the street, white-haired men in faded Guayabera and polo shirts gathered around a table planted in the middle of the broken sidewalk to play dominoes, Cuba's national game. Deep in concentration, they click-clacked rectangular black-and-white tiles, their *fichas,* into position while intermittently throwing back sips of *una colada*, a larger cup of coffee that is served with thimble-sized cups for sharing. The rolling-rain rattle of maracas, metallic clicks of Cuba's rhythm-carrying wooden claves, and bongo beats of son music carried from a front living room parlor to the street, as if on holiday from the country's watchful eye. One gentleman smacked his hand on the table, finishing the game, and the others exploded in a raucous mix of laughter and what I presume were blasts of four-letter words.

In one afternoon scene, there it was. Joy, I noted, was as much an element of Cuba's culture as language. In essence, joy is a choice.

I began to study my new surroundings as a way to find my own joy again. If they could, then why couldn't I?

Mom's illness had redefined me, springing brain circuits loose. I felt broken, and my goal was to walk the streets without being blown over by light winds, feel so much with acute precision. It seemed cruel to feel so much.

Chapter 8

Hallmark Moments

Early July 2000

When I stumbled out of that New York hospital, my hands wouldn't stop trembling. I walked across the street to a pay phone and called my roommate, Jacque.

"Hello."

I couldn't even form words. I think I was only sputtering and gasping.

"Melanie? Melanie?" I heard her say over and over, but I couldn't respond to my own name.

"The doctors had only given her two years to live. How was I going to tell my brother? I don't understand, she was fine. She's my mother. She's only fifty-three. Why can't they DO anything? No chemo, no radiation, no transplants. What the FUCK?" I rambled, Jacque cried. "I have to go, I have to go, I'm sorry," and I hung up.

On the corner was a store where I bought sorbet, two vases with two large bouquets, magazines, and water. I pulled myself back together and went back inside the hospital to see my sick mother. I couldn't say cancer again. Sick was all I could manage. I told Jim to go. He had been there all day and looked awful. Their apartment in the city was nearby.

Mom and I then forced a change in tempo. We talked about lighter things: my job, things going on in the entertainment world. And it was at that exact moment, at twenty-four years old, that my relationship changed with my mother. It wasn't in my mother's nature to dote or to be sappy, but I could see she wanted to tell me something and didn't know how to say it. We always laughed at overly maternal moments, soap operas, and sickeningly sweet television ads, referring to them as Hallmark moments. Continuing to talk on the surface about seemingly mindless topics to rid our brains of the horror of her predicament, she looked me dead in the eye midsentence and interrupted me.

"You know that you and Walter are the best children. I couldn't have asked for more. I love you so much and I am so sorry that this is happening to you."

She was crying so hard she almost couldn't finish the sentence. I fell in to her, cradled her head, and I became the mother.

"It's OK, Mom, we'll be fine. We will be just fine."

Suddenly we heard a soft crescendo of sniffling on the other side of the curtain. We both burst into laughter. We forgot there was another woman in the room and found ourselves in one of our own Hallmark moments. If there is a fine line between love and hate, then there certainly is an equally fine line between sadness and hysteria.

I was there late, until around midnight, I think. When she told me to go home to get some sleep, I agreed and walked out numbly. As I left I heard her begin to cry.

Chapter 9

Advanced Cancer

July 20, 2000

Monday night *Talk* hosted a party for Joe Eszterhas, screen-writer of *Basic Instinct*, who despite all appearances of being a human bulldog, was cordial and even sweet whenever I spoke to him about organizing the event.

The New York regulars were there: Lauren Hutton, Regis Philbin, tons of press people, *Entertainment Tonight*. It was a successful party and at the very least, my two weeks of total insanity, filled with last-minute invites, endless RSVP lists, and party prep weren't completely in vain. On Tuesday morning, physically depleted and mentally wired from too much coffee, I took a cab from work to a 10:00 a.m. appointment at one of the satellite offices of Sloan Kettering. I met Mom and Jim upstairs in the Zen-like room and after greeting both of them, I put my hand in Mom's and directed my attention to the Japanese-style waterfall that was trickling down in front of me, which proved to be the only thing that could tame my caffeine overdose.

I don't think any of us spoke two words. Someone finally called Mom's name and we all got up and walked past the front desk to one of the back rooms. We were waiting on Dr. Bloomgart, whom Mom spoke of almost mystically. She said there was something really special about him. He was a healer.

Whoever he was, I needed him to pull my mom out from under this unforgiving thing that was eating all of us alive. We were waiting to hear results from the previous Tuesday's CAT scan. We were all desperately hoping to hear that her football-sized tumor that seemed to spring out of nowhere was gone. I needed this magician to tell me that Mom had years left, but I was terrified that he wouldn't say what I needed or that even if he did, he might be wrong. We waited and waited and still none of us spoke. My eyes worked the room. Trash, soiled linen, six small drawers, cabinets, Curity pads, Savoy rubber gloves, something that looked like a dentist's chair, a bunch of strange-looking instruments, blue shiny floors, Mom's manicured toes, mine (which desperately needed attention), Jim's Nikes, two purses, and the wine bag, which was always with Jim. The four daily newspapers that he read were in the bag that morning, but it would be replaced with a bottle of crisp, white wine, Brie cheese, and Pepperidge Farm crackers after four o'clock. I heard voices outside the door and sat up straight. The handle turned and the doctor walked in to find three pairs of eyes staring at him intently. Two females in similar white doctor's coats were standing in the hallway, looking in at us.

Dr. Bloomgart came in and gave Mom a kiss on the cheek, shook Jim's hand, and then turned to me. He stared at me a good five seconds before speaking. "You look exactly like your mother," he said, glancing back at Mom and then at me again. "It's uncanny."

I feigned a smile. "I've heard that once or twice before." Bloomgart sat down on the chair and pulled it closer to Mom, his back almost completely to me. He began to talk about the CAT scan and then stopped, abruptly. He craned his neck around to look at me.

"You know about everything with your mom, right?"

"Yes, sir."

He returned his attention to Mom.

"Since you have an advanced cancer . . ."

Advanced cancer, advanced cancer, advanced cancer. I didn't hear anymore after that. The doctor's lovely British accent faded and I was stuck on advanced cancer. I suddenly felt as sterile as the needles in their plastic wrapping. I looked at Dr. Bloomgart and the two other female doctors standing behind him. He leaned into Mom when he was talking to her. He was firm, but he was also very gentle with her. Advanced cancer, advanced cancer, advanced cancer. I was going to throw up, right there on the floor. Just hearing those two powerful words made her look weaker, smaller. Her clothes were four sizes too big by then, but she was actually holding up really well.

He told her that he wanted to do another embolization, which was a relatively new treatment for cancer at that time, in which the medical team inserted an embolus, or foreign object, into her blood vessels to try and "starve" the cancer. Mom cringed. "I was afraid you were going to say that."

"I know it's rough, but you reacted so well to the last procedure. Really gave the tumor a hell of a scare."

She nodded, defeated. With that, he said that he would call her soon and got up and left the room.

I felt so tired all of the sudden, but I pushed out a bright face and told Mom that she was going to get it over with and we'd get rid of that nasty thing. And as we walked out of the room and got on the elevator to go back downstairs, I looked at Mom and suddenly succumbed to a fear so large I had to swallow hard to push the sentiment down. *Was I going to forget my mom one day? Is that even possible?* And if so, what would I do when I needed to hear her voice?

Chapter 10

Devastating Blow

September 6, 2000

It was 9:00 a.m. on a chilly, sun-filled Wednesday morning. I had taken the day off work and was at Sloan Kettering again with Mom. My stepfather, Jim, had had a heart attack the weekend before in Colorado. As Mom said, our typically quiet family had become like a soap opera.

We checked her in for the follow-up embolism procedure. She got into a gown and they put her on a gurney and took her down a long, white sterile hallway. They took my mom away and all I could do was watch.

The good news was that by November we learned that Mom's embolism had worked. The large tumor had died off, but the bad news was that in complete defiance of my family's hopes, five more angry tumors had sprouted in her liver over a four-week period. It was a devastating blow.

I tried to remain positive, but it was increasingly more difficult to keep my anxiety at bay. Though I was kept busy at work with daily tasks, after-work parties, and a side editorial project that I was researching, it was not enough to keep my mind off Mom. At minimum, work was a consistent distraction.

Chapter 11

Old Man and the Sea

Draped hospital rooms were a distant memory when Cynthia and I sat on the marble steps of Casa de la Amistad, a mansion that we discovered behind trees that lined Miramar.

Cyn and I had walked a small marathon that night, searching for this apparent secret spot, whose beauty and perfection took us both by surprise. I could hear music in the distance as we entered the marble-floored hallway, which pulled us by an invisible rope to the back patio, straight ahead. As we walked out into the night again, long branches of fragrant, red flowers hung low, pocketing small tables with three and four chairs each. This was the music I had listened to so many times in New York.

Sitting in Havana, I was in the middle of my CD, living it out loud. I couldn't believe a place could be so beautiful and that this transportation was real, sitting under the stars with a cool breeze, listening to the music that had long soothed me. This was the reason I had sought out this curious country, as if the island itself would trick my heart into beating again for the sole pleasure of dancing to its music.

So far, it was working.

The night was perfect. When Luis joined us, he gave us each a kiss on the cheek and then told me he liked the red fabric rose pinned to my black, strapless dress. His look into my eyes pounded me into the ground, like a hammer.

"Thanks," I said and smiled coolly.

"Red roses usually mean you are in love," he said.

"I'm not in love," I mused. "Just happy to be here."

He put his hand gently on my back and asked where we'd like to sit.

"How about over there?" I suggested, nodding to a spot under the branches.

We spent the night free of much talking, listening to Cuba's notes in the sky.

The next day we slept in and made our way to Maria Victoria's by noon. More confidently we walked up the stairwell in search of our feast.

We were greeted by Maria Victoria, who was genuinely happy to see us. As we walked in, we each received a big hug and kiss. Her husband, Santiago, greeted us warmly and invited us to sit with him while we waited for Maria Victoria to finish in the kitchen.

Somewhat mysteriously to me, Spanish unlocked its secret code and my time in Spain began to pay off. I understood with relative ease as he spoke about his family and asked us about ours. As we sat there for some time, young girls and women of all ages came in and out of the door, heading to the back. I guessed they were family and friends because their leisurely entrances and departures were unmonitored.

Santiago rocked in his chair and asked us what we thought of his city. We loved it, we said. Didn't understand it, but we loved the energy, the people, and the music.

For a few moments, he said nothing and then, "It's sad what's happened to my city."

We sat quietly as he took a healthy pause.

"It used to be so beautiful here," he remembered, staring off into the distance, beyond the balcony's rails. "I feel like we're all waiting for something, but I don't know what for."

I found myself helpless, without words to comfort or change the situation.

We said nothing.

As if on cue, Maria Victoria walked into the main room, stage right, with plates in hand and announced that lunch was ready. The four of us sat and ate the best meal I had had in quite some time. Luis was set to pick us up at 1:30, but I hadn't as much as looked at a clock. Somehow it felt like we should go, so we thanked Maria Victoria and her husband and headed back outside.

Luis sat in his Coco and looked up as we swung open the gate at the front stoop. At the top of the stairs, I looked directly at him. He winked at me and boom, it was like a gun right to my heart.

I smiled, but as I did with any other feelings at that time, I pushed them straight down to my feet and left them on the stairs behind me. I had become the master of pushing away any real emotion before it took hold.

We small talked about lunch and Luis headed out of Havana toward Hemingway's house, known as *Finca Vigia,* or "Lookout Farm." On the thirty-minute-or-so ride, Cyn and I sat still as the midday sun beat down on us. It was textured heat, nearly bereft of oxygen, and felt akin to a giant fly trap. At times the diesel fumes—eye-level in the PAC-MAN–shaped transport—were so overwhelming that we both pulled our shirts up over our noses, like little American bandits. I couldn't imagine how Luis worked in such heaviness all day long, given his obvious affinity for cleanliness—and breathing.

The heat was visible. It swayed, as did the palm trees, leaving the city's center and entering an area with bits of houses, battered shacks, children and chickens, and wooden boats along dark rivers. Mangy dogs in packs and a number without limbs ruled the streets, scattered in wild currents, showing no signs of ownership.

The farther we reached into the suburbs, the more I felt eyes on me. One of my translucent legs hung over the side of the cab. I sensed I was a bit on display, like an unusual bit of pottery, but never threatened.

At a stoplight, Luis turned slightly to the right toward me and touched my ankle when making a point about something in the area. Boom, another shock, this one up the leg, up the spine, to the back of my neck and head. It was a vast shock of goose bumps, one for every freckle on my body.

I studied his profile. He was like a painting with his long eyelashes, his lips, his skin. But I turned my focus hard right, studying my surroundings so as to not look at Luis. No more surprises.

There wasn't a luminous sign announcing the entrance to Hemingway's house. There was only a gate with an old man taking money. For foreigners it was a few bucks to get in and an additional two if we wanted to take photos. Well, of course we wanted to take photos. Good God.

Cyn and I paid our dues and Luis rolled through. We were officially on all fifteen acres of Hemingway's palm- and vine-covered *finca*. We parked under a canopy of mango trees and tropical flowers, and walked under its veil to the front of the house. It was absolutely magical and worth every penny, camera and all.

We stepped up onto a wraparound porch, topped by a trellis covered in a wild spray of colors. The windows were open, but the front door wasn't. I propped my hands in the sill of one and leaned in while Cynthia fixed herself similarly in the one next to me. Like his writing, Hemingway's house was uncluttered and masculine, exuding a rough sophistication. Kills from his hunts hung on the walls, overlooking rows and rows of books stacked and lined throughout the house.

I was mesmerized by the books. My glasses out and on, I stretched my eyes as far as they would reach, but they weren't strong enough to read book titles on the faded jackets.

Luis suddenly appeared next to me and Cynthia quietly moved on. He pointed to items in the house, offering details about the rows of military jackets, boots, and hats in the closet. I only captured pieces, though I nodded in assurance. An English-speaking guide stationed on the porch chimed in, noting that everything in the house remained the same as Hemingway left it in 1960. Other notables: he and his fourth wife, Mary, lived on the property with fifty cats—give or take a few—and he always stood while writing.

We visited *Pilar*, Hemingway's beloved wooden boat, and saw the gravestones for his four dogs. The graves sat clearly marked next to the pool, once blessed, they say, by a naked Ava Gardner.

The "lookout" of "Lookout Farm," a separate building on the compound, gave way to a lush second-floor view. There I studied photos of Hemingway with his muse for *The Old Man and the Sea*, as well as those of him with Castro and in the bars where he sat frequently enough to inspire lyrics from the great Compay Segundo, one of the Buena Vista Social Club superstars.

Afterward we drove back into Vedado to Cristobal Colón Cemetery, the fourth largest cemetery in the world, with approximately 800,000 graves across 140 acres. We parked and walked under the two wide arches of the entrance, built by the Spanish in the late 1800s. I'm not sure if it is fact or folklore, but it is said that the large pass is a tomb for a construction worker who died while building it.

The cemetery is an intricate requiem and has the makings of a small European city, paved with roads for walking and viewing the thousands of elaborate mausoleums, gravestones, and family vaults. Cubans and tourists frequently visit one statue in particular—*La Virgen de La Milagrosa*, or Miracle Woman—who holds a baby in one arm and a cross in the other. She is said to have died giving birth and she and her baby were buried side by side. Yet, when their bodies were exhumed as is done every two to three years to make room for other family members, the baby was found in her arms.

Women go there to pray for their children, or ones they one day hope to have. The *Virgen* is held in such regard in Cuban culture that it is out of the question to turn a back to her. Visitors face her as they walk away, only coming about when they are entirely out of her line of vision.

In those surroundings I could recognize the haunting beauty, but I couldn't appreciate the landscape of tributes for what it was. A heaviness came over me that I couldn't attribute to the pressure of the day's heat.

Cutting a path away from Cynthia and Luis, I wandered alone, feeling like I did in New York City. I had walked block after block after block, barely pausing for traffic, until the tingling that raced up and down my legs turned to complete numbness in the freezing temperatures outside. The cold air on my face reminded me I was alive at all when little else did. Skirting the headstones of others, I retreated deeply inside myself. Tears fell in large, hard drops, leaving a trail on the ground that had long been irrigated by the flood of others. My connection wasn't personal, though it felt that way.

The complete loss of control, the disarray of emotions, felt like an affront to any progress I had made in Cuba. With seemingly no strength in me, I pulled it from the clear, blue sky to find my way back to the taxi where Luis and Cyn were already sitting. Certainly they recognized my chaotic mess, but neither said anything. They greeted me sweetly and we drove off without saying a word.

This was the day Cyn had arranged for us to move out of our hotel to rent a *habitación* from a local couple. A friend of a friend of hers had recommended the ground-level apartment. In a different *barrio*, the vibe of the neighborhood was much more urban. Inside was clean and quaint enough and we were led to a simple room with peach walls and a tall yellow ceiling that helped keep the room cool. Two beds were pushed together and a standing fan scanned the room.

Our hosts were a young married couple, both of whom spoke spot-on English. Karina was a Cuban medical student, as beautiful and elegant as she was bright, and Victor was from Sweden. He tinkered with computers, though I'm not sure what was accomplished, and he made an excellent host.

Luis left us to settle in, but planned to return that night. Victor, a natural comedian, made an outstanding dinner, paired with red wine that swiftly kicked me out of my funk.

By the time Luis arrived, I was in a good mood. He took us to Café Cantante, a small bar with a stage on the bottom floor of Teatro Nacional, Havana's national theater. A young band rocked the stage, mixing up traditional salsa with rap.

Luis told us a couple of times that he didn't dance, which would make him just about the only one in the whole country who doesn't, but he in fact could. He was shy, but could move once propelled onto the dance floor. After much coercion Cyn and I were successful at just that. However, not two minutes later, she once again played her little disappearing act.

Luis and I bonded as dance partners, and as the crowd swelled late into the night, the physical distance between us lessened in increments. The music was very loud, but I never felt the need to talk. The gift of my disheveled state at that time was inherent freedom. I was an emblem of nature at its core, a child who reacted simply and directly to whatever was in front of her. If I didn't want to talk, I didn't. I wasn't concerned if Luis liked me or if he didn't. I didn't care what I looked like or what I said. All was precisely in the moment.

With his face in the cusp of my neck and my hands locked in his, we moved from distant foreigners to friends, and perhaps something beyond, in a full sweep.

We were like that for some time until the band stopped, abruptly, and bright lights swept the room. In a snap, we found ourselves close, nose to nose, and Luis suddenly seemed nervous. I followed suit. We both looked around, anywhere but at each other, and noted something or other about Cynthia. I said that we should probably find her. We broke apart like snapped chopsticks, each taking a step back.

Cynthia found us, asking to go because some guy was giving her a hard time. "Of course," I said, grabbing her hand to lead us out.

Luis drove us back to the apartment and gave Cynthia a peck on the cheek. Sneaky little booger, she bolted immediately, already on the other side of the apartment door by the time my foot touched the street. I aimed to offer my cheek, but Luis kissed me quickly on the lips. I took it like an electric shock, waving good-bye as I scurried inside. I may as well have been fourteen years old.

I didn't know if I would see Luis again, because the next day we were going by bus to Trinidad, a coastal town four hours east of Havana. With little emotion, I simply accepted reality as it was.

Cyn and I crashed hard into bed around four, only to be up three hours later. Our bus ride initially followed the highway through Cuba's interior, bordered by mountains and coconut and mango trees. From our bus perch, we passed clopping horse-drawn carriages and clusters of people with their thumbs out, hoping to hitch a ride.

Victor had warned us that we would be bombarded by throngs of people trying to get us to stay with them, but I had never experienced anything like this. People flashed pictures of their homes, spouting out broken English.

"Good house!" they screamed, these Cuban paparazzi, shining their brightest lights on us, pleading for our business.

Victor had made a call the previous night to find us a place. We spotted a middle-aged man who held a sign with our names, spelled correctly, and pushed through the crowd to reach him. He was Manuel, a hyperfriendly fast-talker. We followed him to his home, deep into cobblestone streets passing freshly painted, bright-colored row houses in the middle of downtown Trinidad. I was overjoyed when I spotted similar birdcage window fronts like those we saw in Havana—blues against peaches and greens against yellows.

Manuel walked us into the front parlor of his home, through the small kitchen and out the back door. A courtyard stairwell led to our aquamarine apartment with matching fan. It was tiny, but clean and efficient for our needs.

I looked out of the window and onto a mosaic of terra-cotta rooftops that stretched as far I as I could see, with palm trees sprouted between houses. *I miss you, Mom*, I thought. *I miss you so much I can't breathe. But I am free, free, free on this little island.*

We stayed in that night and sat at a private table set up for us in the courtyard. While an old-school tape recorder played Cuban music, we dined on two enormous open-faced grilled lobsters, served with potatoes, green beans, and a cucumber salad. Under the stars, we talked and laughed our way through mounds of rice and beans and pieces of divinely sweet fruit.

This was heaven.

The next couple of days, Cynthia and I wandered the streets of Trinidad, talking to locals along the way. For one entire day, we basked in the sun on a nearby beach. We walked the white sand

and played in the crystal waters, but for the most part we sat, quietly. I tried to read, but couldn't focus, rereading line after line, so I returned to my healing zone, eyes closed, taking in the sun.

At some point we made our way to a beach shack, covered in palm fronds, where we bought pizza and margaritas. As we took our spots at the lunch table in full sunlight, a woman sat in my line of view with her back to me. She was forty-five, fifty, maybe, with blond hair cropped just above her neck and a frame that resembled that of my mom's.

Behind my sunglasses I squinted in the sun and in the blur she became my mother. I watched her nibble her food and sip her drink. At times she turned her head, pushing my mom's profile away. But then she would go back to her original pose and I, too, returned to a world with my mom in it. Four months without my mom and I was desperate to see a glimpse of her, even a distorted one.

Surely my cheeks would have flashed bright red, had my face not already been covered in freckles exacerbated by the sun. I felt pathetic in my own desperation and didn't tell Cyn of my mind game. I carried on a conversation with her as normal, but my soul continued a simultaneous and emotionally charged game of charades.

When a waiter came to deliver our pizza, I snapped to. This was ridiculous. How could I be so weak? I was twenty-five years old, an adult, and needed to buck up. *Be strong, Mel*, I told myself. Yet, any chance I could I found myself returning to the same indulgent delusion. After some time, the woman stood and leisurely walked off.

I was furious. "Stay!" I wanted to scream.

Instead, devastated, I helplessly watched her trail toward a hotel in the distance. I didn't say a word to Cyn and asked her if we could go back to the beach. For the remainder of the day, I lay in the sand and only walked briefly up and down the beach.

That night, in the middle of town, we found Casa de la Musica, an open-air venue with live music. It was pure freedom under the stars, in a sliver of a town on that strange, little communist island where we danced with the locals for the better part of the night.

Chapter 12

Path Finder

After four days in Trinidad, we decided to head back to Havana. The bus trip should have been four hours, but inched closer to six. Our driver stopped to talk to people on the highway and then to buy pineapples. This would have annoyed me in New York, but in Cuba I found it funny.

We got back to the station in the late afternoon. As we stepped from the bus, there he was. Luis. I was happy to see him. He got out of his taxi and came over to us and kissed each of us on the cheek. While near the station after dropping a client off, he stopped to look for us. He knew there was one daily arrival from Trinidad, though he had no idea when we were getting back, because we hadn't either.

It wasn't until much later that I found this somewhat unreal. We had crossed each other again, in a city of three million, but it never occurred to me that this might be a path.

Chapter 13

Signs and Symbols

My mother died four months before I traveled to Cuba. She had been sick the seven months prior to that.

Fitful images of her, jagged and crude, flashed in and out of me with no warning. Particular visuals singed the most: deeply jaundiced skin, yellow as a canary, a swollen belly, a diminishing jawline with pronounced teeth, making her look like a biology class skeleton, and her face wincing in pain as she sat under the lightest setting of the showerhead. As her skin broke down just before dying, my handprint fossilized into her arm and stomach, where I gently touched her, fading only after some time. It was pure science fiction.

Just two weeks after her death, I had returned to the pandemonium of New York. We were in the throws of organizing a conference that would bring literary giants, scholars, the world's top political, business, and military leaders, as well as Hollywood's biggest and brightest, together for outdoor breakfasts and round-table discussions at Bacara Resort in Santa Barbara.

I had been ordained as the official daily task keeper and detail manager. There were invitation drafts, redrafts, and quadruple redrafts, never-ending lists, directions, and phone numbers to be obtained, mailings, a barrage of phone calls, arranging of cars, flights, and hotel rooms, as well as catering to Hollywood requests, which became more bizarre by the day.

My patience, already wearing thin in fathoms, played hardball with a sense of professionalism that I tried to maintain in the wake of my mom's absence. Typically assistants phoned in with specific needs for their bosses. However, one late afternoon a well-known type called directly to ask if he could acquire the money that the magazine was going to use to purchase a first-class airline ticket for him, though he was going to fly out on a friend's private jet. I paused and thought for one moment he was joking, but then realized he wouldn't waste his time personally calling upon a magazine assistant if he were. The tone of my voice mustered importance, but it was far from real.

I told him that I couldn't make that decision and I would have to filter his request to Tina and the others.

Another call came from a powerhouse of a star who specifically requested that the room have no caffeine products, no oysters (as if we would strategically place them around the bed as little aphrodisiacs), and no Evian and Perrier bottles. Some other water brand was requested and even more specifically, asked to be placed on the mini bar, on each bedside table, and in the bathroom. The bed's head also had to be elevated exactly six inches.

One asked for M&Ms in the room. Not too unreasonable, I thought. However, then I learned that all blue M&Ms had to be removed from the stash. Apparently, my grandmother wasn't the only one who let superstition rule.

As the calls increased, so did my anger. It was all so ridiculous. My mother fought so arduously just to live and here was Hollywood losing sleep over candy colors and raw seafood.

I did my best to focus on work that began early and went late into weekday nights. I tried to keep it together, yet I was more unsuccessful by the minute. The coils inside me were springing. Numerous times through my workday, I shot into the bathroom near my desk and fell apart, sliding down the wall and onto the concrete floor. I sobbed, just short of a wail, until there was nothing left in me. Numbly, I gathered myself, flushed my face with cold water, and put on my reading glasses in an attempt to hide red, swollen eyes.

Almost nightly, I dreamed about tsunamis so real that I would wake all but leaping from my bed. In them I was always protecting children, usually my young cousins, and once our family dog. The waves never fully covered us, but their force and close proximity were enough to yank me from the deep caves of my heavy sleep hours. Awake, I would lose it and be overcome with an impossible sense of helplessness.

In defense, I took up yoga. My friend, Allison, had recommended a class taught by Janti, a tall, lithe Brazilian man with wild, curly hair pulled back into a ponytail that sat high on his head.

I have never been particularly good at yoga because I am seemingly made of concrete instead of human tissue. Even as a young gymnast who competed statewide, I had to work harder than the other girls to do splits. Perhaps that is why Janti's physical agility astounded me. As one of his pupils—shoeless and covered in spandex, and waiting to be transformed—I wedged into the small studio, which sat two floors above the madness of West Broadway. I think everyone in the class wanted to be just like him. He bent and contorted effortlessly, until he resembled nonhuman shapes like pretzels, butterflies, and Kama Sutra scribbles.

Janti's almost two-hour classes were more vigorous than any advanced aerobics class I had managed in college. Despite the level of difficulty I had in achieving poses and keeping up with the

Olympic pace, I was inspired to twist and turn my body in ways I didn't even know were possible.

The deep yogic breathing was our platform. Somewhere in Internet literature I read that Westerners tend to breathe incorrectly, focusing on the in-breathing, as opposed to the out-breathing.

As Andre Van Lysebeth explains in *Yoga Self-Taught*, "All good respiration begins with a slow and complete exhalation, and that this perfect exhalation is an absolute prerequisite of correct and complete inhalation, for the very simple reason that, until a receptacle is emptied, it cannot be filled."

For so long I took in my mother's illness, trying to absorb her pain. The toxic mess was still rattling inside me, like residual oxygen that was no longer beneficial to the body. I needed to be emptied before I could be filled with life again.

I knew back then that those Saturday morning jaunts in the brutal winter months were not merely about wringing out stress, but also chasing away demons that had me in a headlock. I lost myself in the sessions, taking Janti's commands like a prophet's, attempting highly uncomfortable positions. On occasion I surprised myself as I (a) got into the position and (b) held it for the long one, two, three seconds.

We also did headstands and handstands, which I had not attempted since my gymnast days. At twelve, I was the leader in the informal handstand competitions we held at state meets, but that failed to come into play more than a decade later.

What I like about yoga is being in the moment. Though difficult for me in many aspects, I found that the focus on inner strength was vital to me at that point. My life was intense and I had to fight back intensely.

At the end of class, we rolled to our backs as the lights went out. In near darkness, the room was silent and we were able to process our bodies' cycles, what we had just accomplished, and to continue the notion of being in the present. At that time, my "present" was unbearable. No longer having muscles to exercise or poses to consider, I became vulnerable, overexposed, and, without fail, I would cry. Tears rolled down the sides of my face and dropped on the floor. My relaxed state released toxins buried deep inside me for months. It was scary to confront the emotions head-on, but I tried to focus on the deep breathing and pushing the flow of oxygen to my broken heart.

Janti came to each of us and gently pushed our shoulders down or used his thumbs to press on our foreheads. I was so raw that I could feel the slightness of his fingers in the tips of my toes, as if he were tickling them in unison. After composing myself, I changed clothes (as spandex was not the height of sophistication on New York's streets) and visited Dean & Deluca next door.

One morning following my yoga retreat, I wandered the food aisles, looking for something healthy to eat. I was particularly frail, knowing I would have to go to back to work two days later. Back in the city after a brief trip home, the world was in full motion, but I hadn't caught up. Yoga was my retreat to feel quiet and safe from New York, which was empty to me. I couldn't go anywhere without looking for my mom. She was on every corner, every display, every crème brulee I smelled and every crevice I walked. Mom was New York.

As I stood in the checkout line with fruit and water in hand, a middle-aged man in front of me turned and did a double-take. Ugh, here it comes, I thought, some stupid pick-up line and I thought it was apparent to any and everyone that I was in no mood.

"Excuse me," he said. "You look *exactly* like someone I know." (His overemphasis on the *exactly* annoyed me.)

Come on, go away, I thought. I imagined porcupine needles pressing through every pore in my body. *LEAVE ME ALONE, LEAVE ME ALONE, LEAVE ME ALONE,* I repeated in my head.

But he didn't. "It's uncanny," he said, all but shaking his head in disbelief. "You look just like my friend, Marti Bowden."

It felt like the subway underground smashed into me. My knees unhinged.

I looked at him, right in the eye. "That's my mom."

"That's crazy. That's totally crazy." A pause, then: "How is she?"

For the first time, I had to say it and there was no easy delivery. Coldly: "She passed away. Two weeks ago."

My chest tightened, I became light-headed, and I thought I'd knock out on the spot. The guy looked horrified.

I don't know what he said and I can't remember his name or how he knew her. I only wondered, out of the eight million people living in New York City, why did I have to bump into him?

Deepak Chopra suggests in his teachings that nothing is random—that our lives are full of signs and symbols. What hidden dimension of my life had been unlocked, and why was I a better person for that encounter? That never was clear to me.

Chapter 14

Castro the Artist

"Cuba is a surreal painting and Castro is the artist," Victor told us that night at dinner. "Everyone thinks he's a politician, but he's really an artist with installations and shows."

This came following raucous laughter that halted to a standstill, as another Swede, Inar, who had joined our group at the apartment in Havana, relayed his most recent experience in Cuba.

Inar was in his early twenties and a good-looking, laid-back kind of guy. Humor rolled off him in a natural, light way, even when translated into his almost perfect English, making it easy for him to crisscross cultures. All of us, including a sweet, young Frenchman named Andre, who also had arrived that day, repeatedly laughed out loud.

The six of us were seated at a wooden table made for eight, in a room that was pleasantly small and infinitely happy with bursts of bright colors painted by Victor himself. Our meal was exquisite, one that Victor had pieced together in no time, it seemed. We had good red wine, though I never knew what it was we were drinking. We were eating and laughing with mostly strangers, and yet the energy in the room became intimate, as if we had all traveled the world to find just this place, only to meet one another.

We had all been laughing so hard that the tempo finally slowed, if for no other reason than to breathe. Following the pause, Inar began to tell us about the trip he had just taken to a western region of Cuba called Pinar del Rio, where tobacco is harvested and rolled into Cuba's iconic cigars.

He told us that he and a friend had rented a car to drive out of town and on the way picked up a young Cuban guy looking for a ride. They, too, joked, as Inar spoke some Spanish. Not long after a policeman's sirens pulled them over. All attention was directed immediately to the Cuban in the backseat. He was drilled as to what he was doing, where he was going, and why he was with two foreigners. Inar didn't understand his response, but whatever he said was useless; he was dragged out of the car and pulled behind a building that sat off to the side of the road. Inar didn't know what had happened, but felt sick, and only could drive away. His face was uneasy retelling the tale. Shortly after, he said he was approached by a mother who offered her daughter as a bride, like a distressed but lovely Cuban token, as she rallied for a better life for her child.

On the plane ride to Havana, I had read stories like his and other odd details about Cuban life, such as the fact that lobster and birthday cakes were illegal for Cuban consumption, but not for foreigners. I didn't dare ask the couple who had served us just that in Trinidad, though the thought crossed my mind.

American travel books also noted that the Cubans can't enter hotels, their restaurants, or pools. The Internet was off limits. I was aware that emails I sent from the Hotel Nacional were monitored in some fashion and certainly no Cuban could afford the one-dollar-a-minute fee charged at the hotel. I knew that letters and packages from the US would never reach our new friends in Trinidad, as Cuba has no functioning postal system.

It was difficult to decipher what was real, what was true, and if each Cuban shared the same existence. If so, did they accept their fate or simply fear their reality and therefore succumb to it? Did they even consider another way of life?

The only person that I could really look to to answer my questions was Luis, but I didn't feel like I had the right to push my curiosity on him. Yet, somehow I managed.

One night, after a broken conversation about different places in the world, I asked him if he likes big or small cities. He replied, simply: "I don't know."

I felt like one gigantic ass. How could I be so naive? I was so selfish talking about places I've seen, things that I do on a routine basis at home that he couldn't do (or hadn't done?) at all. I wanted to apologize, but I didn't. I clammed up, unable to redirect the conversation.

I didn't know the rules. Had he not traveled because he didn't want to or because he couldn't? I was afraid to ask so I didn't. He appeared unbothered. Or was he complacent? I didn't know, so I sat there like a fool, unable to form words. I was terrified I'd say something idiotic again.

Only one distinct thought remained.

I had traveled to this country to feel free, ducking real life and American laws to go to the forbidden land, only to become muted. I did feel free from responsibility and reality, for only a short time, I knew, but not being able to talk about politics or ask questions, and being acutely aware that I could only say so much, made me crazy.

A new sensation came over me as I suddenly felt unusually patriotic about my own country. Living in Spain and visiting other countries, I forever found myself apologizing for being an American. Frequently, I was compelled to explain that Americans are compassionate human beings interested in the rest of the world and that we do dine on more than fast food. We didn't all vote for Bush.

In many instances foreigners told me that I wasn't like most Americans who visited their countries. While I was content to be accepted by my new peers, I was equally annoyed for the preceding reputation. I assured my new friends that many Americans are just as open as I am.

Sitting across from Luis, I was overwhelmingly frustrated for him. The light and intelligence beaming from his eyes told me that he was underwhelmed living the way that he was. There was something too controlled under that calm he carried. I sensed that he only needed a new platform and he could soar.

I didn't know if he was happy or unhappy, but I didn't feel I could ask him that either. To some extent he answered my question as we sat at an ice cream shop under neon lights. His twin sister, Anabel, married young and moved to Brescia, Italy, and Luis had petitioned the Italian embassy in Cuba for permission to move there.

He did want more.

Chapter 15

Good-byes

Two days before we were to go home, Luis came to meet us at the apartment. Cyn and I wanted to go to the beach and he suggested Playa del Este, which is about twenty-five minutes outside the city. He didn't have his taxi that day, so he summoned a private car with an affixed taxi sign.

However, ten minutes in, midcity, he asked the driver to stop so that we could get out. We had no idea what was going on, but followed him. Back on the street, he quickly hailed an official, government-sanctioned red taxi so that our first driver wouldn't have any problems with the police, he told us. Tourists paying a driver of a privately owned car equates to free enterprise, something that can create a host of problems in Cuba.

We were dropped directly on the beach's white sands, overlooking a stunning vista of aquamarine waters. Luis paid the driver, buffering our attempts to do so. We walked a short distance to put our towels on the sand and kick off our tanks, shorts, and flip-flops. As we settled in, a well-armed military guard in the distance began to walk toward us.

My throat swelled, and I was crazy nervous for Luis. Was he going to be in trouble? My mind raced, remembering the story

Inar had told us about the kid getting dragged out of his car. The policeman stopped, staring hard at us. I was frozen in terror.

The man asked Cynthia and I where we were from, unaffected by our response. His attention turned to Luis, who was asked the same. Luis's reply was met with a hasty response: he needed to give the officer his ID.

On the surface Luis was calm, but by then, breakfast had worked its way to the top of my throat. He handed him his ID, which Cubans have to have on them at all times. They spoke back and forth without any emotion in mumbled, terse language. I didn't understand a word.

The officer handed the card back to Luis and walked away.

I couldn't help it: "What did he want?" I asked Luis.

"*Nada*," he said, dismissively.

What do you mean nothing? I thought, but didn't say. Instead I respected his quietness and simply replied, "OK."

I was angry, really angry, that Luis had to live that way, absolute power always presiding over him. But I was also suddenly over-joyed that he might soon be with his sister in Italy.

My nerves calmed and we all enjoyed the day immensely.

That last night in town, Luis invited us to go to his house to have a drink and then go out. In her last matchmaking effort, Cynthia accepted the invite and then later declined, as she and Inar were going to go out on the town together.

Victor answered the door and called me. When I came to the front parlor, Luis was sitting on the sofa. He smiled when he saw me and got up, tapping my cheek gently with a kiss.

I had dressed in a black V-neck, paired with white pants that only allowed the tips of my black heels to peep out. Long, pencil-like silver earrings hung crisply from my ears, nearing the tips of my shoulders. My pale skin had turned two shades darker since arriving in Cuba, virtually erasing mounds of freckles that hid beneath.

He was in pink. His dark skin played against the color that so many men from home wouldn't touch. The shirt was balanced by light linen pants and European leather slippers.

I introduced the guys, but the dynamic between the two was uncomfortable and I quickly noted how unfriendly Victor was with Luis, in stark contrast to his behavior with all of his guests. I couldn't figure that one out because Victor, of course, was married to a Cuban.

Cyn cut the ice, bounding in playfully to say hello. She said *adios* and we were off to Calle L where Luis lived with his mother, Ana.

Luis easily flew six flights up, whereas I was embarrassed to be a bit out of breath. I regularly climbed my share of stairs in New York, but this was a killer.

On the top floor of the building, a long balcony overlooking the Malecón bordered our walk. As we reached the second-to-last door, Luis pointed out the American consulate, located inside the Swiss embassy just below us. A racing thought: *What would they do if they knew I was here?*

The two-storied apartment was not terribly different from that of Maria Victoria's, where we had eaten lunch our first week in Havana. The granite floors were clean and the dining room table was made of solid wood and marble. Two armoires filled with chotskies—bits of religious this and mundane that—took me back to Spain. The Spanish woman I had lived with also collected numerous items and put them on display.

Ana, a beautiful woman in her late forties, sat on the sofa, smoking.

I noticed something inherently elegant about her, just as I had with Luis, though she was dressed casually. However, unlike Luis, she was exotic and inaccessible in a way that he wasn't. I had no idea what she thought of me, only that I must have been as foreign to her as she was to me. I sat on the opposite end of the sofa and tried to make small talk with her while Luis went into the kitchen for drinks.

I was uncomfortable, even though Ana was friendly and seemingly open to my broken bits of Spanish. Cynthia wasn't there to fill in gaps or transform my mishaps into coherent sentences. It was just me in a stranger's home in Cuba.

Luis turned the corner, rum and Cokes in hand, his pink shirt draped on his arm. A bright, white undershirt in its place played against the darkness of his skin, making it all the more pronounced. My soul floated, barely touching anything in its path, but my reaction to him was visceral.

He got it, a wink buried in his smile.

I must have turned a shade of hot pink, thankful for the shroud of burned skin that masked my embarrassment. Yet, my eyes stayed with his. He handed us each a rocks glass, based with a linen napkin, and pulled a chair up to sit directly in front of me.

"Mami, she's so pretty, isn't she?" he said, never moving his eyes from me. He called me *Pecosa*. Freckles.

I flashed like a bulb again and quickly changed the subject. I wanted to know why Victor had been so rude to him back at the apartment.

"He thinks I'm only with you to leave the country," he explained.

I was horrified. "Why would he think that?"

Prejudice among their own exists greatly in Cuba, he explained. Victor assumed that Luis was there to find me, an ultimate escape from his country. At that point in my life, my entire existence was raw, childlike, and clean in its accuracy. I knew there wasn't one contrived bone in Luis's body. He was as pure as I was in that sense.

Soon after, we left to listen to live salsa. Again we danced for most of the night and again we connected, but I took the moment for what it was and not what it could be. I would return to Mexico the next day.

Our final day in Havana, Luis met us at our apartment and hailed a cab bound for the airport. Cynthia and I were quiet, digesting our trip and brief evolution within the boundaries of another country and culture.

Riding along the Malecón, the driver pointed to a house buried in the thick green of a side street, noting it was one of Fidel Castro's fifty-two houses. Cynthia asked the driver to stop so she could take a picture. Walking up onto a large median in the middle of the street, she raised a large lens, focused, and snapped. Two armed guards immediately rushed to her side, bantering, questioning what she was doing. They didn't take her camera, but I thought they would.

In the car Cynthia kept her camera to her side. Our mental images would be all we would carry with us from that last ride in the city. Presumably, there were no good or bad parts of Havana, just everything in shambles. No one can unravel a culture in a matter of days, but I felt as if the Cubans, who manage a level of grace and dignity in the midst of it all, were lost in the mix.

As we rode along the coast, the cab driver toyed with the radio until he was able to tune in to a Miami station playing Barry White. He sang the US National Anthem, and Cynthia and I remained quiet, neither of us commenting on the huge irony. But perhaps she quietly respected our own country a bit more than before, just as I did.

At the airport Luis asked me to call him when I landed in Cancun and to email him from home. He would be in Italy within six months and maybe we could find each other again, he said. Six months was so far away and this friendship so seemingly out of the realm of possibility that I graciously accepted his words and inherent sincerity, but my heart couldn't fully buy into the notion. I didn't even know what I would do when I got back to Savannah, much less six months later. And really, I wasn't sure he'd even remember me much by then.

We said our good-byes and I was genuinely sorry to leave. Able to sense a bit of humanity again, the thought of returning to the real world was bitter.

Chapter 16

Therapy in the Garden

I landed in Savannah, moved by one country, only to be completely lost in my own.

My family blanketed me with love and support, but the impact of life without my mom was still overwhelming and unreal to me several months out. I couldn't get past the fact that I couldn't pick up the phone to talk to her; I couldn't catch the train to Convent Station, a short drive from her house. I missed her voice, her silly little jokes.

My brain wanted to go north. An article that I had pitched and worked on vigorously disappeared, never finding the pages of *Talk*, but I still had a job there when I got back from Cuba if I wanted it. Tina had made that clear to me herself. After my exhaustive efforts at the Bacara conference, I had mini-impromptu conversations with a couple of the magazine's senior editors, standing in the middle of the open office landscape, with discussion of me assisting one of them. I was finally touching the corner of my dream, to work in magazine editorial, and Tina Brown's no less, but after my mom died, staying in New York became more difficult by the day.

I was in the office on a late spring afternoon when my dad emailed to check on me. I told the truth. I was a disaster. My insides burned, the concrete hurt the undersides of my feet, night-time was terrifying, filled with nightmares of my faceless mother, but it was especially harsh to wake up each morning and remember that she was gone. His response was simple: "Come home," he wrote. And I did, only a few weeks later.

I desperately wanted to return to New York after coming back from Cuba and felt pathetic for not mustering the strength to do so, but my heart told me no. I was still experiencing stress, which had rooted itself firmly in the city. The tsunamis were back, and on top of it, I began to wake in the middle of the night, gasping for breath, as if I had been forcibly held underwater thirty seconds too long. This strange new pattern took during the day, too. In the middle of ordinary activities, I caught myself holding, holding, holding followed by a desperate push of breath.

I didn't know what was going on, but it was unnerving. I missed my yoga teacher, Janti, and took to the deep breathing techniques he'd taught us. It helped a bit, when I focused heavily on it, but it wasn't enough. I needed help. Yoga was the most logical answer to me so I flipped the pages of our local paper for classes.

On a Tuesday morning I met a friend at a B&B on Forsyth Park, the Central Park of Savannah. By then it had been some time since I had last twisted and stretched, but my surprised muscles and arteries adapted and finally loosened enough to let me dig into the chaos of my body. I didn't experience anything close to the intensity as I did in my New York jaunts, but I felt physically relaxed and emotionally drained following the class. I asked the instructor, who was named Judy, if she had a minute after everyone else had left.

"Of course," she said and sat with me on the floor, cross-legged, her hands resting on her legs.

Judy's energy was soothing and I enviously wondered how someone could be so peaceful. She remained quiet and waited for me to speak.

"I've been having this weird thing happen over the last month or two," I said finally.

Her kind gaze held firm.

"I keep holding my breath and then use the deep yoga breathing to try and shake it. But I don't like having to think about breathing."

"First of all, don't dislike thinking about breathing," she said. "Most people don't think about it and they should."

Very gently, she asked, "Have you been going through something recently?"

I looked at her, I bore into her, and all of a sudden I couldn't talk. I literally couldn't open my mouth. She didn't take her eyes off me and after some time, I nodded yes. Tears started to fall in large drops, welled up in full buckets behind my eyes, and then burst outright as if they had been stored up for years.

"Melanie," she said, as she put her hand on mine. "Breathing is a symbol. There's something blocking you."

I stared at her.

"Something you don't want to move past."

I stared at her. I swallowed hard.

"You're not ready to move forward. There's something you want to stop."

I nodded and tears streamed uncontrollably. I was a blubbering mess and I felt ridiculous.

"It's OK, it's OK," she said. "I don't know if someone has died or a family member or friend is ill, but whatever it is, you're not ready to move on and it's OK."

These were Chopra's signs and symbols, I just had to pay attention. I had no idea that my body was speaking to me. In fact, it was screaming at me. All I had to do was figure out what to do with this indecipherable language that beat its drums and screamed its anthem trying to communicate with me. I had punched it down for so long.

Soon after, a dear family friend, who was my mother's contemporary, invited me to her house. Quickly, she recognized the scorching fire inside me. Just before I left her house, she handed me a piece of paper with a therapist's name on it. She didn't push me on it, but mentioned she was going to call the woman's office to say that I might make an appointment. For the first time, I considered getting professional help. This was huge for me. At that time, I didn't easily accept personal defeat. I thought I was invincible.

Following a quick trip to New York to gather the last of my things, I called the therapist's office and confirmed an appointment. Overwhelmed, I sat hollowed and terrified of revisiting what I wanted so much to clear out of my mind.

The counselor's office, as I predicted, was uncomfortably foreign. She came out, shook my hand, introduced herself as Sue, and led me to a floral explosion. I sat on the flowery sofa, which sat against flowery wallpaper, and looked outside to a pocket of trees surrounded by flowers. A cat, looking frazzled and singed, rubbed up against the sliding glass door. We were all but distant cousins, sitting opposite each other.

Sue was short and blond with large eyes and a skirt that fell above her knees. Her voice was raspy and distinctly Louisiana Southern.

She sat down in a chair across from me and said that she wanted me to tell her why I was there. Quiet and still, she waited for me to begin. I thought, in my great twenty-five-year-old maturity, that I would be highly efficient. Dig in, get out. She was going to make an assessment, give me some tools, perhaps, and I'd resolve lingering issues. Really I was OK, I just needed a cleanup.

Boy was I off-base. In a shot, my heart railroaded my brain, flinging all logical thought processes out the window. Wild and powerful tears poured from me like lava burning down my cheeks, following two choked words, at best.

I was an idiot, a weak, weak idiot. Other people cried. Other people lost control. I was stronger, or should have been. And Sue, I didn't even know her. At that time, I was insanely possessive of my mother's memory and didn't like to share her with many people. There was the blue leather Nike bag I snagged from Mom's Morristown home and filled with the new size eight jeans she happily slipped on in the months before she died, her gray Yale Drama School and Florida Gators T-shirts, and her extensive Playbill collection, which was stationed in the northwest corner of my New York bedroom. The gold, six-paneled Japanese folding screen that once divided my mom's first Manhattan studio acted as a barrier between her things and the rest of world when I was away. And her large, black dress coat, one size too big for me, only escaped the hanger in my closet for her memorial service. I wrapped myself in it like an adult-size swaddling blanket that she had left only for me.

Yet, in spite of myself, I started to talk, in between my slovenly gushes of emotion, and apologized repeatedly for the endless waterworks. The more I spoke, the more I seemed to regress. Feeling like a large, metal plate was compressing on my chest, I was touching dangerous territory, falling into what again felt like deep, deep despair. The gauze I had put over my heart, just so, to fend off emotional invasion in the wake of my mother, was ripped off, reminding my just how exposed my wounds still were.

I sat in the therapy garden, not wanting to talk, but I told myself I had to or it was pointless to be there. I was told that taking power away from my memories and from my mother's illness was the way to win the war I never wanted to fight. So I began. I was scattered, bouncing from one point in time to the other. I didn't know how to make my thoughts flow. I felt robotic and totally and completely erratic.

It turned out that Sue had lost her mom to gallbladder cancer seven years before I did. Her mother's experience had been similar to mine. The swollen stomach, disparately attached birdlike appendages, and the disturbingly sulfuric-tinted skin color that forced my mom to have to think about her looks for probably the first time in her life—it was all very similar. I know she told me this so that I might find comfort in her empathy, but I only felt worse.

Half an hour in, I was completely gutted. Yet, I went in deeper. I touched on the moment—and the second I opened my mouth to say it, I wished I hadn't, but it seemed there was no turning back—when I sat in the living room with Jim, as they rolled my mother off, zipped in a black, plastic bag. That image haunted me most.

I meandered further into the deep blackness of the night that I thought I lost my mind. It must have been only a day or two after my mom died. The memorial service was a couple weeks away in New York and I was going to go home until that time, but Jim needed people around him and there were things we needed to take care of so I stayed a few more days. Together, we closed her bank account while acid burned inside me. We addressed envelopes for the service and cleaned her closets.

I held firm until we hit her bathroom drawers, a rumpled mess of her makeup and half-used jars of concealer, brushes full of her blond hair, bobby pins sprayed in and around, and perfume that nearly sent me over the edge, with her scent so firmly embedded in the mash.

I wanted to run and scream, get out of the house, but at the same time, I carried overwhelming guilt in leaving, as if I was going to make our good-bye final. It felt like abandonment. Somehow staying in her house and in the immediate bi-state area that included New Jersey and New York, where we spent so much of our time, I wasn't really leaving her. I attached myself to her absence, her void, as if that was a real person in and of itself, with permission to exist only within Morristown, the theater districts of Manhattan, and the railways in between. This thing, this black snake, curled into me like a sick child, weaving a mutual existence.

In my black hole, how was I going to find my way in the world without her or the void, that was, in fact, my lifeline? It was all I had left of her. So when that void attacked me, I didn't know where to turn.

One night, alone upstairs and unable to sleep, I crept down the stairs, presumably toward the kitchen for a drink of water, in almost complete darkness, save a sliver of light from the cracked door on the second floor. Jim snored loudly below.

Down a handful of steps, my mother screamed at me. Actual, clear, real screaming, which sent me into a state of petrification.

"MELANIE, MELANIE, MELANIE," she wailed, her voice shrill, in pain and running from death, much like a real episode that occurred a couple of nights before she died. Lying on the sofa in the room adjacent to her hospice bed, I ran to her, as did my stepsister, Leanne, who was trying to rest with me.

My mom sat up, her face horribly distorted, screaming for me over and over, gripping the bed's side rail. She flailed her arms around, fighting demons that I couldn't see or touch. She was fighting death, fighting not to lose us, and hurting in a way that I could never imagine. I tried to calm her with touch and the sound of my voice, but nothing could tame the force of nature that pushed her.

Suddenly, she dropped back to her coma-like state and I was stumped, hanging in midair, without a landing strip for my torrential flight of fear and confusion and anger that compounded by the moment.

Leanne put her hand on me. "I'm sorry," she said. "I'm so sorry."

I broke, shaking so hard I could not steady my hands. I don't remember the rest of the night.

But on this particular night, the night she screamed at me in the darkness on the stairwell, there was no one to run to, as Leanne had gone back to Germany for two weeks. In my tunnel Jim seemed miles away. Only my mother's hysterical voice in the dark and the void, that sharp-edged absence, was attacking me.

"MELANIE, MELANIE, MELANIE!"

My heart raced, yet I remained in total paralysis.

She did it again—"MELANIE, MELANIE, MELANIE!"

Boom, a voice of logic kicked in, directing me with internal militant instruction:

GO BACK UP THE STAIRS.

Still too scared to move, I was lucid enough to know I was teetering between the sane and the insane.

TURN AROUND AND GO BACK UP THE STAIRS, my general directed, sternly.

THIS ISN'T REAL, he said. THIS ISN'T REAL. GO. GO!

I gripped the handrail, finding a brief moment of relief in the solidness of the wood under my hand.

My mom screamed again: "MELANIE, MELANIE, MELANIE," sending every membrane, cell, and hair follicle on my body into salute.

The General: GO NOW, MELANIE. GO NOW. THIS IS NOT REAL. THIS IS NOT REAL. GO UP THE STAIRS! NOW!

I took orders, snapped, and broke free of the rail, clumsily plowing up the stairs. In the bathroom I flipped on the light and turned the shower on. As scalding water ran over me, my eyes closed and I imagined a wax shield that would protect me, but it never formed. I sobbed, bent in half, not sure I was going to get through the night. How could something hurt so much?

At some point, deflated of tears, of energy, and of emotion, I stepped out and slowly wrapped a towel around myself, in half an effort. In the bedroom, I put on soft clothes and turned on the overhead light, as well as a lamp, and fell into bed, soaking my pillow with a mop of heavy hair. I turned on the TV for an added layer of protection against the silence of the night. Finally, my exhaustion won and mercifully, I didn't wake up again until there was full sunlight.

As I digressed from that memory, I realigned myself to the bright room where I sat. I told Sue that I had no idea what had happened on the stairs, but I had touched the unimaginable. It was the most terrifying thing I had ever experienced, next to losing my mother.

Sue had remained completely quiet, a dedicated listener, as I navigated my way in and out of my personal war. When it was clear I had nothing more to say on the subject, she spoke. She began using words that could have come out of my own mouth: primitive, animalistic. "You're amazed that you didn't die feeling like you did."

I nodded in agreement, too tired to talk anymore. I knew I had to dig in to come out, but re-waging a battle I had barely survived the first go-round seemed counterintuitive.

In my sudden overexposure, an immediate need to have soft things on my skin, to eat warm food, and to be enshrouded in hot water took over. Having none of these things near me, I fought the urge to pick up the cushion full of flowers next to me and put it to my chest.

As I sat crumpled in front of her, Sue asked me how I felt then, eight months after my mom had died.

We talked about my breathing issues that I still couldn't fully decipher, despite the yoga teacher's point about blockage. Why couldn't I move on if I knew that Mom was gone and she wasn't coming back? It had been eight months and I was a big girl, wasn't I?

Sue told me that often your brain knows the truth, but your heart can take a while to catch up.

"I'm supposed to be the strong one," I said. "Not my younger brother."

And I thought, but didn't voice: *I hate feeling so helpless, I hate missing her as much as I do, and I hate that she isn't here to talk about New York, the Twin Towers coming down, and the beginning of the theater season.*

Carefully, Sue said that I could be dealing with post-traumatic stress or possibly even a mild depression.

NO. This was an immediate auto siren, and I became very defensive of the latter. I didn't want to hear that I was depressed. My mom was dead. I was grieving and to me, in my nonlicensed opinion, there was a difference.

She treaded lightly, noting that some people do well with medication for a short time, to even out everything in the brain that can go haywire under extreme circumstances.

Sternly, I said no again. I'd rather talk, scream, and cry it out. She understood and didn't say another word about it. The hour was up in a flash.

I didn't like or dislike Sue. The experience was difficult and scary, but good or bad I didn't know how to assess. I left the room and made another appointment because I thought I was supposed to. I told myself I needed to follow up and push my way through the sludge. I needed to be OK with what had happened. I needed peace.

On the way out, I made another appointment with the receptionist, who graciously noted that they could help me with the cost, since my insurance didn't cover mental health. Those two last little words ignited a torrent of internal floggings; I berated myself for not being stronger as I signed a medical billing document.

I never did go back, nor did I call to cancel the appointment.

Chapter 17

Gypsy

Without any idea of what I was going to do, I picked up work at a restaurant through the summer months and into early fall. I still wasn't brave enough to return to New York, and I didn't want to be in Savannah long-term. My thoughts turned to travel.

I'm project-oriented so I was happy to collect and save money I earned from long hours waiting tables and opening expensive bottles of wine, rather than spending it on after-dinner drinks of my own. I picked up more shifts at the restaurant with the idea of moving abroad.

My family probably credited this to my semi-gypsy ways, but, also, it was a sort of last homage to my mother, who in the months before her death told me that her only regret was that she never lived in another country and never learned another language. Imagine, out of all life's lessons, those were her missed opportunities.

Much like my process before going to Cuba, I inadvertently latched on to the richness of another Latin city—Buenos Aires— through its music and dance, specifically the tango, which I find insanely luring. I rented movies, read articles, and was sold quickly. I booked a ticket for January 2002.

I wasn't concerned about how I would live in Argentina. I'd figure it out. Besides, I had a little money left to me from my mom and fifty thousand Delta miles that Becky, my second mother, gave to me, tied with a thick ribbon of sympathy.

My family had their doubts. What was I going to do when I landed? Where would I live? Could I make money? Was it safe?

My father, whom we facetiously refer to as the professional worrier, didn't grill me. Later I heard from family friends that he was calling anyone and everyone he knew with connections to Argentina or South America to ask all of those same questions. But he gave me my space and let me make my own decisions, as he always has, in his quiet way.

As I planned my trip and became more excited, I wondered, as I had several times in the previous months, if Luis was in Italy with his sister. If so, why hadn't he been in touch? My gut told me he was sincere and that he would call or write to me when he could. Yet, what I couldn't figure out was why he continued to circle in my head months later if I wasn't interested in him.

Chapter 18

Freckles

October 2001

Luis sat in one of two wooden rocking chairs in his living room, staring out of the window.

His mom walked in the room and watched him for a good sixty seconds or so.

"You're thinking about Freckles, aren't you?" she said.

Luis turned toward her and smiled.

Chapter 19

La Americana

Two weeks later

I don't know why I picked up the phone to place the call. I could barely speak Spanish anymore, but it was as if I was on some screwy form of autopilot and I couldn't put the phone down.

Shit, shit, shit, the phone is ringing. My heart raced.

"*Dime,*" a man's voice said.

Ahh, ah, ah, I wanted to hang up, but didn't.

"Tell me," is how his answer literally translates, and this sounded so rude to me at the time.

I asked for Luis.

The man spoke very fast, but I was able to pull short groupings of words: *Él no está aquí* and *dos semanas.*

Luis isn't here and two weeks. What did that mean? I asked if he was in Italy.

"No."

"OK, thank you," and I hung up.

I was shaking, but I knew that I would call back in two weeks.

***

The end of October

Luis picked up the phone, in a near whisper.

"*Hola.* Luis?"

"*Sí. Quién es?*"

"This is Melanie, *la Americana* . . ." Dying, I was dying.

Beyond that I don't know what I said specifically, but he answered in short bits. I had made a terrible mistake in calling. He wasn't interested in talking to me. What was I thinking?

In an uncomfortable linger, waiting for the moment to hang up and never call again, he said, "I'm glad you called."

"You are?"

"Yes."

His shyness dominated for some time, but eventually he opened up as we began to email and call on occasion over the next three months. I learned that the Italian embassy had denied his visa for no apparent reason.

Internet access wasn't easy for him. He had to go to an office where he knew someone and pay one US dollar every time he wanted to use the Internet. I did the math based on Cuban salaries and knew that was a lot of money.

Our exchanges were casual and brief. I never put much emphasis on where they would lead us. I was still excited about going to Argentina. By early January, however, Buenos Aires was a fiery mess. Corruption and political unrest had escalated into riots. The country plowed through five pundits in two weeks and fires plagued the city. The reality of a severe economic depression became all too real as I watched clips of angry citizens, wrapped around city blocks, demanding their money from banks.

My family and friends inundated me with emails and phone calls, pleading with me not to go.

Adventurous I am, but stupid I'm not.

Airlines released identical statements that all tickets to Argentina would be refunded. I had time to reroute. My father suggested that I talk to a friend and customer of his who has business interests in Budapest, Hungary. We had lunch. He told me how exciting the city had become with its people, the opera and classical music houses, the bath houses, and the food. I left intrigued.

Not a week later, my brother connected me with a friend of his who attended medical school on the outskirts of Budapest. We all got together for dinner and it was a virtual repeat of the conversation I had days earlier. That night I went home and called Delta to change my ticket from Buenos Aires to Budapest, set to leave in March.

Those in my immediate group were a little stunned when I mentioned the formerly communist city, since I had no real connection to it, nor had I talked about it before. I explained that while my thoughts were to go to Paris after Argentina fell, I thought it might be interesting to venture into unchartered territory.

Luis thought it sounded interesting, though he knew little about the country himself. Then he asked me if I might want to visit Cuba again before I left for Europe.

I paused.

Why not? At the time, my world sought any direction remotely appealing to me.

We planned for a visit in February, as I was first going to an all-girls orphanage, Las Rosas Pequeñas, or the Little Roses, in Honduras. This was a gift from my sweet aunt Jane, who offered to take me on the trip with her and a small group from her church. My aunt Margaret gave up her spot and handed it to my friend, Zia.

Within the group of missionaries, their own acts of kindness were aimed at me. In what was staged diversion, the trip would overlap the one-year anniversary of my mother's death. My aunts never said a word, but I knew this was their intent. I accepted the invitation, welcoming the chance to be in a different environment during that time.

The second week of January 2002, I found myself on a plane, much too early to be awake, with a fantastic sunrise that painted the path to Honduras. There were twelve of us ranging in age from twenty-one to seventy, including Aunt Jane, Zia, and me.

The orphanage's compound was surrounded by a twelve-foot concrete wall, topped with barbed wire. Armed guards opened the gate for the van, which had collected us at the airport. We were greeted by the school's founder, who offered a simple, but decent meal. A brief roundabout told us about the school and home for about eighty-five young girls who had essentially been tossed away, as is frequently the case, she said. This was at that time the only orphanage of its kind in the country, with all others designated for boys.

Though it may not have been evident to the naked eye, many of the girls had horrific childhoods. One girl, Marta, had lived in an apple crate for eighteen months and drank only coconut milk. She was too small for a seven-year-old girl. Tania was abandoned twice; others were forced into prostitution as young as five and six.

Despite it all, the founder explained, the girls were playful, spirited, and always open to visitors. They were being raised with love and care by fellow Hondurans and volunteers from around the world who were taking year-long sabbaticals with room and board as their only pay. Most of the orphanage's funds were provided by donations and fund-raising efforts. The school's founder spoke around the world, which was how she had found my family's church.

As we walked up the flight of stairs and onto the platform at the entrance of our living quarters, young girls in their school uniforms played outside with a green-mountain backdrop. Inside, the main room was simple and clean with a table and chairs, sofa, TV, coffeemaker, and a few magazines. Two bedrooms were outfitted with four sets of bunk beds. One bathroom shot off the main room. I was reminded of a slightly more adult version of the North Carolina camp where I once worked as a counselor.

The next couple of days were spent getting to know the girls, who were exactly as the director had described—lively, fun, and nearly exempt from any outward appearance of difficult past experiences. They were excited to be with us and quickly invited us into their games, their meals, and their computer stations, equipped with slow dial-up. The older girls liked to write to past visitors in the United States and were eager to practice English.

It was only when salsa blasted from boom boxes inside the gymnasium that I sensed something of a past. Some of the girls, no taller than my knee, were as skilled with their moves as the Cuban women who danced in Havana's nightclubs. It was a type of sexuality I had never seen in such small children.

Zia, who was the only young male on the trip, became a virtual campus rock star. Disturbingly mature sexual advancements, betraying the girls' stick figures and ponytailed innocence, emerged as they aggressively pursued him. At one point we had to hide him in the apartment after they chased him around the compound.

Friday, January 18 was a spectacular morning. The foliage of the mountains was faint but apparent, as the peaks had been swallowed by deep, vast clouds.

Little birds, no bigger than my thumb, sat along the compound's wall edge in front of me and tweeted wildly. Eileen, a lovely English woman with us, told me that the melodious blackbird was the one making all the noise. A bird book in hand, she excitedly offered details about the yellow-bellied bird and his friend, a bananaquit she thought, who flurried in front of us and took their places on the barbed wire.

When we returned from morning play with the girls, one of the women in our group who had stayed behind was watching CNN. I sat on the couch to watch for a moment when the reporter announced that Tina Brown's *Talk* magazine had officially folded.

In a solid stroke, it was fast rewind to New York with its ups, downs, and the doors that had opened and closed there. There was my devastation at leaving *Talk* and New York and the sudden demise of my future that had been stolen from me. I had felt like a failure when I left. My life was thrust outside Manhattan's publishing world, the epicenter of my universe. Or so I thought at that time.

Yet, as I listened to commentary about presumed reasons for the magazine's downfall, I felt surprisingly removed from that time in my life and for all the emphasis that I had placed upon it. Now I was in the middle of Central America, one day before the year anniversary of my mom's death, and my perspective was no longer one-dimensional. My New York experience was not a dead, hallowed dream that would remain unfulfilled. Instead, it was part of my development. Tina Brown and my friends at *Talk* were also moving on. In an instant, I didn't feel so isolated in my experience.

With validation, a chapter in my professional life closed peacefully in simple bananaquit surroundings.

A few days later, I went home grateful for the trip and for the chance to be in a different setting on the anniversary of my mom's death. Being with the girls, who chose to laugh and play and learn despite all they had endured, gave me strength and appreciation for what I did have. Like the girls, I didn't have my mother, but I did have a vast stable of love and support.

When I got back to Savannah, I did laundry and repacked, this time for Cuba. Six days on the island and then I would head for

Europe to look for a job that would carry me after my mother's small inheritance ran out. With no calendar, no clock, and no future to speak of, that was all mine to create.

Chapter 20

The Kiss

It wasn't until I descended into José Martí Airport that I began to physically shake.

What am I doing in Cuba? Alone!

Visiting a man I knew little about was a stretch, even for me. Ever the independent American, I insisted to Luis that he didn't need to pick me up from the airport. I would take a cab. When I arrived at his house and climbed six flights of stairs carrying a heavy suitcase, I was sorry I had succumbed to my feminist ways.

I was exhausted and out of breath by floor six and paused at the top of the stairs. I hoped my flushed cheeks and 3-D freckles would return to normal before stepping through his door. Slowly I walked the long hallway until I reached the slightly familiar door to the apartment, which was wide open.

I hesitated. Again, *what am I doing visiting a man in Cuba, whom I barely know?*

Yet, there I was. I walked in and saw Luis's mom, Ana, on the sofa and another young woman rocking in a chair. Ana stood up and came to give me a kiss on the cheek. I suddenly realized that Luis's sister, Anabel, whose photograph I had seen on my first trip, also was in the room. She glanced at me and looked away.

I had made a mistake. Luis was nowhere in sight and this was a terrible, terrible mistake. Ana motioned for me to sit in the rocking chair so that my back faced the door. I nodded and sat down, just after pushing my large suitcase to the wall.

Quiet. There was an awkward, long quiet. Ana offered coffee.

"*Si, gracias.*" Espresso was perhaps not the most idyllic drink for me at that particular moment, as my hands wouldn't stop trembling as it was, but it would give me something to do.

Anabel got out of her chair and went to the kitchen.

Ana spoke to me and I didn't understand much. She tried again, I sorted out the best I could, and replied in choppy *español.* Anabel brought in the delicious coffee, but after two sips I was finished and put the doll-size saucer and cup on the table in front of me.

I nodded my head at Ana. "*Gracias.*"

"*Por nada.*" You're welcome.

I smiled, she smiled. I took a deep breath and grinned again. I realized that I was vigorously bouncing the back of my right knee on top of my left leg and I put my palms over my legs to curb the nervous gesture.

A voice was suddenly behind me at the door. I looked back and it was Luis, who was wearing shorts but no shirt. He was very tan and his hair was all over the place. Contrary to his put together demeanor, it was apparent he had been at the beach.

I stood up and smiled. He came straight to me.

"*Hola,*" and he kissed me on the cheek. He smelled like sand and beach and sun. He looked like the sun. He was, in fact, more strikingly handsome to me than before.

"How are you?" he asked.

"*Bien,*" I said, which was a total and complete lie.

His Spanish continued at a deliberately slower pace, though this would not be the case with anyone else in Cuba.

"Come on, let's go upstairs, you can put your bag up there. You get my room."

"OK."

He grabbed my suitcase (with tremendous ease, I might add) and jumped up the stairs, skipping every other step. His room sat off to the right at the top of stairs.

"I'm going to take a quick shower, OK?"

"*Está bien,*" and I nodded, relieved to be upstairs and not in the pressure cooker below.

His shower was fast indeed and he walked into the room in a pair of jeans, as I sat on the bed.

Luis went to the closet to look for a shirt. His hair was pushed back. He was one of the most handsome men I had ever seen. I had to tell myself it was OK to breathe. I told my heart it had to pump.

He asked me how my flight was, if I got to the house easily. "Yes, fine," I said in my best efforts at Spanish. Much to my chagrin, I knew that my Georgia lilt would never completely disappear.

"Your Spanish is much better than I remember."

I looked down at the bed. "Thanks."

"You didn't talk very much the last time you were here."

My eyes shifted to him: "I know."

I heard footsteps coming up the stairs and Anabel appeared with a tray full of cheese, fruit, and sweets.

She plopped down in front of me. "*Quieres?*" she asked.

Would you like some?

"Yes, thank you."

I was surprised by her newfound interest in me. Maybe it had been her nerves, too, downstairs. But whatever it was, it was gone and she was suddenly very pleasant.

I picked up a cracker with cream cheese and guayaba, a local fruit that is often made into a thick paste and used as a dessert. It was delicious, but I was embarrassed to say so.

We were all quiet.

"Do you want to go for a walk?" Luis asked, sliding a short-sleeved, red Lacoste shirt over his head.

He wore the color powerfully and it caught me off guard. I nodded yes as a surge of energy shot from my chest into my ears. Worried that I might emit a flashing signal if I appeared too eager, I sat very still in my attempt to express confidence and composure.

Frankly, I was thrilled to go walk and do something, anything, that didn't solely rely on language. I followed Luis down the long flight of steps and outside. We walked side by side to the Malecón, where waves crashed over the sea wall and sprayed into the street.

Eventually we stopped walking and Luis popped up on the wall in a quick hand catapult and then brushed his palms together to clear off any mess. He extended his right hand, which I grabbed firmly, trying not to slip from his grip, as I propelled up with my right arm and pushed from my left hand, stationed on the rough concrete surface.

The gray top was cool on the underside of my legs and as we turned toward each other, I carefully folded and looped my legs, ending in a semi-slouched lotus pose. There were fishermen scattered among the black rocks below us and it had just gone dark, but there were a few distant streetlamps that gave us a few light streams to see each other.

"Nervous coming to Cuba?" Luis asked carefully.

I nodded yes.

"I was shaking through passport control," and lifted and moved my hands in show. I wasn't entirely sure he understood my Spanish and the physical gestures offered backup. "Luggage took a long time, but once I got outside it was OK."

"I can't believe you're here, in front of me," he said, his eyes never swaying from mine.

"I know, I know. *Es loco*," I returned.

There was small talk about going to the beach and possibly the western countryside, Pinar del Río, as I studied Luis's lips, second-hand interpreters of Cuba's rhythmic and slangy words. I told him about home and my family in Savannah, as his hands moved to the tops of mine and then slowly wound around my palms in a warm, cocooned grip. I felt safe when he touched me and my body decompressed in an instant.

His face brightened when he talked about his four-year-old son, Luis Jr., or Luisito, who had moved to Guatemala with his mom, Arasay, just before I visited Cuba the first go-round.

Arasay became pregnant with their child when they were no longer officially a couple. Their four-year relationship already had ended but things happen, as they sometimes do with exes. Though they weren't together anymore, Luis was exceptionally good to Arasay during her pregnancy. She moved back in with her parents in Santa Clara, which sits in the middle of Cuba, about four hours outside of Havana. For those nine months, Luis visited her every few weeks and brought her cold pickles and chocolate that she craved. They cared greatly for each other, but weren't romantically compatible and never would be, so they chose platonic affection.

In Cuba, where many men openly father multiple children with multiple mothers, oftentimes while married, I knew Luis was different. He had always been different, growing up with his mom and twin sister, who dragged him to parties all throughout high school. Allergic to crowds, Luis roosted on outdoor steps, waiting until Anabel was ready to go home. He was always protecting, filling a paternal hole.

His father had left while he and his sister were still in the womb, not even six-month-old fetuses. Luis Sr. had been with their mom for two years before he up and left one day without notice. He had been suffering from an almost fatal head injury that happened while he was at work.

He was lucky to be alive, but he was never the same after that. He started drinking, became despondent, and wasn't interested in working anymore. Pair that with demons from an abusive past, at the hands of his father, Macho Simón (his real name, no joke), and perhaps Luis Sr. was never headed for fatherhood.

History or not to blame, he left Ana, who cared for two small children in a five-hundred-square-foot space in roughed-up Central Havana.

Consequently, Luis knew from a young age that he would one day become the father he didn't have. So while his new infant's mother, a musician, traveled the world for the first three and a half years of their son's life, Luis cared for Luisito alone. He was up at all hours of the night, warming milk, changing and hand-scrubbing cloth diapers, which were boiled and hung out to dry on a clothesline. While Luis worked, his little one—bottle in mouth—rode shotgun through the potholed streets of Havana, ushering passengers to and from in their taxi.

On return, Arasay requested to take their baby to Guatemala to live with her and her new husband. Luis conceded. Increasingly, in Cuba, whenever Luisito had caught sight of a woman who remotely looked like his mom, with ashy blond hair and reading glasses, he would reach out to her and call her mama. But just after his baby boy left, Luis's hair started to fall out and knots in his stomach kept him awake at night.

The day that I had met him in the Cocotaxi, he was as lost and out of sorts as I was. He was, in fact, hiding when Cyn and I found him, eschewing tourists by parking in a non-eventful spot that time of day.

As we sat for hours, cars swerved around the last stretch of the Malecón, lovers combed and played with one another in humid, evening strolls, and fishermen threw lines around us; we had become the only two people in the world under the faded streetlamps.

Luis leaned in and his peaked cupid's bow briefly shared a narrow space with my slightly parted lips before he cupped my face with his hands, looking directly into my eyes and running his fingers back into my hair. When he kissed me, it became my first kiss. The only kiss. The one that devoured culture and language and challenged everything I knew about life. My heart opened and my soul unlocked, folded into Luis on the crux of that long wall in the middle of Havana.

I felt calm in a way that I never had before. The crushing twists and turns and mess of nerves that had owned me for two years let go, with virtually no effort. For all of my yoga and crying and screaming, tossing and turning, and steeps in scalding water, none of it had managed what time with Luis did, on Castro's isle of all places.

In a brief pause, we cut our conversation and returned to the apartment to change clothes, eat, and make our way to the nearby Jazz Café. Delirium ensued, as we carried on in our escalating and hyper interest, barely noting another soul, though the music hotspot was brimming with people.

We shut the bar down around two or so and walked to the Hotel Nacional to carry the night as long as we could. As a national, Luis wasn't allowed in the touristy spot, but friends who worked at the hotel let him slip in without notice. In the back garden, we rambled on until the wee hours. Crutched under his arm, I fell asleep briefly, as did he, curled into one other. I opened my eyes into the bright of the lights that glared against the still dark night just steps from us. Chattering of the birds signaled that morning was on the rise, but I had no idea what time it was. I certainly didn't care. I was buried in the smell of his chest and rooted myself further, wrapping my arms around his torso. He stirred, returning the gesture. I was so happy that I could have burst.

Together, we gathered ourselves and opted for a cab for the short ride to his house. I all but crawled the six flights of stairs and just before I crashed hard, Luis whispered, "*Te amo.*"

I love you.

Chapter 21

Thirty-Six Hours and Counting

L uis managed to get up for work the next day. It was near
noon when the muted sounds of footsteps climbing the stairs
woke me up. The bedroom door opened slowly and Luis peeked
in. I smiled at him as he came to sit on the bed. He ran his hands
through my hair. I touched his arm, which was warm from the sun.

"*Buenos días,*" he said.

"Good morning," I returned.

He asked me if I slept well. I did.

Did I want to take a shower? Yes, very much so.

He said he would heat the water. Luis went to the bathroom
and grabbed a metal bucket, which he took downstairs and filled
with water from a large white sink sitting just off of the kitchen
area. He lit the stovetop and I waited ten minutes or so for the
water to warm.

As he came around the top of the stairs, his arm muscle flexed,
balancing the weight of the bucket. He held the searing handle
with a potholder and carefully poured half of the steaming water
into a pink plastic container inside of the tub.

Now standing in the doorway of the bathroom, I watched Luis
run cold water from the spout, which coughed and choked, but

eventually produced a light stream. If the water was too hot, then I could add more cold; if I wanted more hot then make sure to grab the pot holder. There was a plastic cup on the side of the tub for rinsing. The pink towel hanging was for me.

"OK, thank you," I said, smiling.

He kissed me on the forehead while giving my hand a light squeeze and said he'd be waiting downstairs.

As I poured the warm water over my head, I began to feel guilty for my showers at home, which frequently ran a good twenty minutes at a time or longer if I was hungover. In that case I would lie on my back on the tub's floor and let scalding water run over me. As the water became lukewarm, I used my foot to crank up the heat until there wasn't any left. Utterly shameful.

When I was in Spain, the hostess with whom I lived asked me to please limit showering time to ten minutes max. I didn't get it. It also annoyed me slightly that the water pressure was weak and the water didn't heat well, but there in Cuba, I suddenly understood. The way I lived at home wasn't the norm; it was the exception. I had never thought of waste of any sort until standing in that drafty bathroom bathing my twenty-six-year-old self with a bucket and cup.

With water an issue in their house, the toilet wouldn't flush most of the time. I was horribly embarrassed later that morning as Ana gently asked me to place used toilet paper in the pink weaved basket on the floor. She had requested this of me the day before, but my habits got the best of me. I felt annoyingly American, but had learned my lesson.

I descended the stairs in a blue halter dress and flip-flops with my hair pulled back in a ponytail and saw Luis and Ana talking at the dinner table.

Luis stood up and pulled a chair out for me to sit next to him. Ana asked me if I'd like coffee. I let out an emphatic yes and she laughed her great laugh while making a round-trip to the kitchen and back. She handed me a doll-sized saucer and cup with her coffee in it, and I took my time sipping.

A plate full of various sorts of crackers, bread, cheese, and fruit sat on the table and I picked at the mango first. It was by far the sweetest I had ever tasted. I then tried a thick slice of Gouda, an expensive and somewhat rare buy in their marketplace. I knew that they were spoiling me. Gnawing on the Dutch cheese, I was reminded of my mother, who used to say, "Gouda is Good-ah" and then laugh at her ridiculousness. Inwardly I smiled at the absurd memory and missed her at the same time. But still, I felt calm and happy next to Luis.

As he had to go back to work, he asked me what I'd like to do.

I wanted to go to Café Paris in Havana Vieja to write and listen to music. Maybe I'd walk around a bit. He warned me that it might not be a good idea to go alone, but my independence (and hard head) still firmly in place, I politely insisted on going.

We hopped in the Coco, which was parked in the driveway of the underground garage. As Luis drove off, I sat directly behind him and he reached back around his bucket seat and rested his hand on my ankle. My thoughts returned to my first trip to Cuba when his touch sent chills up my spine and it was no different this time, only now I embraced the sentiment.

When we arrived I got out, anxious to know when I would see him again. He said he would stop back by in a couple of hours.

I passed my time in the crowded, popular café, set in motion by a two-piece band and female singer. I was seated against a wall with peep holes to the street and my body moved to the music as I studied the other people in the room, all of whom were tourists. I watched, I wrote, I sipped my drink. Looking out to the street, I could no longer turn an eye to the distinct pattern of too many young, beautiful Cuban women, hand-in-hand with decades-older European and Canadian men. The prostitution I tried so hard to ignore flowed freely in and out of hotels, restaurants, cafés, clubs, and the beautiful beaches nearby. There was nowhere to hide from it.

Another massive fallout during the Special Period, prostitution had become a new sort of international tourism following the Cold War. Prior to that, Cuba was handed four to five billion dollars in yearly Soviet subsidies, allowing Castro to provide quality health care, education, and basic consumer needs to citizens. But when the aid dissolved in 1989, times became desperate, as Castro hadn't diversified the economy. The US embargo didn't help matters either, and food was suddenly and severely rationed, so much so that Luis later told me that even if you had money to buy items, there was nothing—not even a cold drink or ham sandwich—on the streets or in the markets.

To this day any Cuban I've ever met tells vivid stories from that time. One of the more eye-opening ones is a tale of cardboard and condoms, which were pounded, shaped, and topped with cheese and any other remotely consumable item and sold as 'pizzas.'

Absorbed in my surroundings, I jerked at the touch of a hand in my hair and swiftly turned to see a man peering at me as his skinny fingers stroked the back of my head through the latticework.

"*Hola, rubia,*" he said.

Ugh! I gathered my things quickly and moved to the opposite side of the room where there was a solid wall. Sitting next to me was a baby-faced redhead, freckled from head to toe.

Within moments, a tall, thin *mulatta* (the ultimate Cuban beauty with her roots split between mainland Europe and Africa, as slaves were once common trade on the island), moved in for the kill. This was territory that she clearly manned.

Little clothing covered her parts that stuck out in all the right places and she slid into a chair next to him, amplifying her assets. The guy bound upright, perfectly aligning his back with the wall behind us. Without saying a word, she pushed her fingertips into his "Guide to Cuba," flipping the pages one behind the other, while she twirled her hair in her front two fingers of her other hand.

His eyes darted around the room, once at me as if in a plea for help, and avoided eye contact completely with her. Yet she persisted, pressing her body onto him. She whispered something in his ear. His jaw clenched. Finally, he turned completely so that his back was to her.

If the situation hadn't been so sad, it would have been interesting in a Discovery Channel sort of way. She seemed unaffected by the cold shoulder, stood up, and moved her advances elsewhere.

I scribbled a journal entry and eventually wandered outside, where I sat on a bench to draw passersby. I am not an artist, but I have on occasion enjoyed drawing light sketches of my surroundings, as much as a creative outlet as a reminder of where I have been.

My pen never lifted from the page as I inked an outline of policemen who stalked the cobblestone rows.

By the time Luis arrived, I was giddy like an idiot. He came to see me several times throughout the day, each visit outweighing the previous one. I thought I might explode having to wait until that night when we could be together, uninterrupted.

After eating one of Ana's divine creations that night, we went to the Hotel Nacional. We sat on a white wicker sofa and watched peacocks strut out from behind the bushes lining the granite floor. Tiny birds flew from one rafter to the next and a trio of musicians played only feet from us. The music, however, faded to background as Luis and I submerged into a world of our own, void of any and all things around us, with the exception of a waiter who stopped to take drink orders.

Our energy was electric and it was within those thirty-six hours back in Cuba that I was able to answer that glaring question—*Why was I here to see a man that I barely knew?*

Luis was the man I would marry.

The thought wasn't really a thought, but more like an extraordinary sense: precise, swift, and sure. Luis was it. I had hopped on a plane, alone, to go to an island that both scared and exhilarated me. Somewhere deep within me, I knew exactly what I was doing. Or I couldn't stop thinking, maybe it was my mom who did.

From there nights rolled into days with no coherent sense of when I had arrived, nor when I would leave. Luis and I were so ensconced in each other that the thought of the latter was incomprehensible.

Luis worked one day on, one day off, while I counted the minutes until I would see him again. He stole moments throughout his workdays and raced the stairs to see me; I leaped into the hallway before he touched the door. We were teenagers again, unapologetic in our delirium.

In his off hours, Luis shared Havana with me from the front seat of his red VW Bug that we released from its padlocked cage in the garage below. We visited Bosque de la Habana, a dense urban forest with sweeping vines that look they might carry you away in the nook of their limbs, and the front steps of Universidad de La Habana, the oldest university in Cuba. Luis pointed out the faded blood stains of Julio Antonio Mella, a university student and Castro revolutionary, which remain like a lost Rauchenberg, abstract in its tell-all brushes of the 1959 uprising.

Driving past the Palacio Presidential, Luis pointed out bullet holes that lace the building like Braille nods to former President

Batista's final stand. Skimming the various neighborhoods this second time around, I noted the beauty and curves of the city's trees, which define it greatly, much like Savannah's do.

For lunch we parked at the end of a broken, concrete walkway and stepped into the foyer of Los Amigos, one of the few legal *paladares* (privately owned restaurants run out of Cubans' homes) in Havana at that time. It was comprised of a handful of tables that were draped in red and white checkered paper cloths.

"*Sientense,*" a large, friendly woman told us as she pointed around the room to suggest that we could sit anywhere we'd like. We were there at an unusual hour, maybe three or so, and didn't have to compete for space at one of the more popular places in town.

Luis pulled my chair out for me and touched my back lightly as I sat. I quickly ordered fresh orange juice, fish, black beans, and rice. Luis added to that tostones, which are plantains that are boiled, smashed, fried, and then sprinkled with salt, as well as *plátanos fritos*, their more mature, sweeter sisters, smashed into divinity.

Moments later the same woman brought out our drinks and a basket of sliced and toasted Cuban bread, butter generously applied. A salad of chopped lettuce and tomatoes with oil and vinegar on the side followed, but Luis suggested that I stay away from any food that was cleaned with tap water. That time, I took his advice with heed. Nibbling bread and eventually plates of food that arrived shortly thereafter, which we cleared almost in full, Luis and I dabbled into the future.

"Maybe we could meet in Italy," he suggested.

"I can check into work visas for me, but can you get there?"

There had already been three denials for an Italian visa for no reason. I was skeptical.

"I'll talk to a lawyer friend. He might be able to help."

He rested his hands on mine over the table. "You could always come here. Stay with me."

The air in my chest cut short. "What would I do? How can I be here legally? I need to be here legally or my family will freak."

"I know," he said with a nod. "Maybe as a journalist . . . or as a student at the University of Havana."

My breath clipped. It was scary to think about being in Cuba indefinitely and falling harder for someone who may or may not be able to get out of the country.

And unbeknownst to us, Cuba and the United States were gearing up for an all-out war as Castro and President Bush were on their way to becoming bitter archenemies.

Chapter 22

War

Two weeks after saying good-bye to Luis, I landed again in José Martí Airport. The day following my return to Savannah, I booked a ticket back to Cuba for fourteen days. I then changed my ticket to Budapest from March to April, explaining to my family that the brief illness I had following my trip to Cuba was the reason for the change.

Yet, my father knew better. He wanted to know who this Young Man In Cuba was that I was going to see for a second time, just two weeks later.

"He's just a friend, Dad," I responded delicately, sensitive to his concern. Still, it was hard not to smile at the mention of Luis's name.

He was silent for a moment and then asked if I could tell him something about Luis's family.

What could I say that would make any sense? He is from a communist country, but he is not a communist. He comes from a broken home and moved out at sixteen, only to move back years later. He is a taxi driver, but an entrepreneur at heart, picking and selling avocados at age six so that he could surprise his mom with the much-needed coins. Forget that Luis and I are from different planets; he is wise and strong and I learned so much from him without him ever trying to teach. He's incredibly bright, kind, and makes me feel safe. He's dignified in a country where dignity isn't easy to preserve. He doesn't speak English, but our connection is strong. He understands me in a way that others haven't before. But how could I tell my dad that my instincts were taking the lead? How could I tell him that I had found the man I knew I was going to marry?

I didn't have to. My father knew all too well.

I sensed his uneasiness, but he respected my decision and never tried to talk me out of going to Cuba again. It is only today as a parent myself that I can fully appreciate his restraint.

Though he did make his point that it had not been his choice to go to Vietnam and never again would he go to a country with a dictator in charge. He would never take the chance of being controlled by one man, even if for a brief stay.

Days later, I trembled my way through Havana's passport control, answering questions about my stay.

"*Estás sola?*" the official asked me.

Was I traveling alone?

"*Sí.*"

He started to flirt with me. I fumbled my way out of needing any assistance in Cuba and pushed through the door, rattled even further.

In near torture, I waited for my bags for over an hour. As I exited the building, mobs of people formed a barrier on all sides, but on clearing to the street, I saw Luis off to the right and fled to him. I dropped everything and wrapped myself around his neck.

The next two weeks were electrifying. We had again become regulars at the Hotel Nacional, and in my love stupor, I still struggled in Spanish to fully express all that I wanted to. Yet, even in my subpar attempts, Luis got me.

None of it made sense. We should have been a complex system, he and I, but together, we were the most natural thing in the world. Luis took my crude slices of Spanish and more than once cast a net around them, creating some semblance of meaning. He was poetic, in fact, in his return delivery of jumbled words.

I studied him. When Luis flagged the bartender and stood to pay, his gestures were elegant, his stance confident. There was a contained power about him, as he spoke with directness, respect, and a gentle shell. He reminded me of my father in that way.

The sun had already come up by the time we climbed the stairs to his apartment. I didn't even feel tired, but knew I needed to sleep. To the bed I went. Two or so hours into my coma-like state, erratic pounding on the door downstairs jolted me awake.

Luis quickly gathered me, as I was in a pile on the bed, and shoved my unruly suitcase into his closet, which he then closed firmly. I was too incoherent to ask what was going on and he said he would explain outside.

Outside? Why do we have to go outside? I thought, but didn't say. "I'll tell you in a minute, come on."

I didn't actually say anything, did I? I was so confused.

"Come on," and he gave me a kiss on my head while giving me his hand to guide me down the stairs.

I had managed to put on some sort of decent clothing and Luis was in shorts and flip-flops. Ana, unflustered, looked like a twentieth-century movie star descending behind us in her long robe, cigarette box and lighter in hand.

We stood in the hallway just outside the front door while noxious gas poured from all of the surrounding windows, both in our building and neighboring ones. It appeared that an enormous fire was taking over the city, but no one was running. In fact, everyone was quite calm.

What the hell is going on? I thought.

Neighbors greeted one another, like any other morning or afternoon. They yawned. Within minutes they were laughing and telling stories. My brain hurt; I didn't understand what was happening. Was I participating in a rare episode of *The Twilight Zone* or some Cuban bloopers show?

Ana lit a cigarette. Probably not the best time to smoke, I noted to myself. Luis then explained to me that the clouds were derived from diesel gas used to fumigate a particularly lethal batch of mosquitoes in the country. The fumes filled the house, yet there was no way to fend off the intruder. My clothes reeked of it, as did the sofas and cushions, towels, and sheets throughout the house.

I wanted to tell Luis that at home helicopters buzzed above the streets, unobtrusively in the early-morning hours while we slept, without even a hint of its haze, but I didn't. There was no reason to make a point about something he didn't have.

My coughing outbursts morphed into laughter with the others, as we celebrated nothing more than life in all its insanity.

A few nights later, Luis and I went to a piano bar. A Cuban Jay Leno-type gave an opening act for the singer, which in its entirety revolved around the Fumigation, and I was happy to understand the inside jokes.

When it was time to leave Cuba again, we didn't talk about the fact that I still had a plane ticket to Hungary in the following weeks. We didn't have to. It weighed on us heavily. He didn't understand why I was going. I didn't understand why I was going, though I pinned it on my mom, saying she had left a small sum to me and I would use it in her honor, living and traveling in Europe. On paper, that sounded good.

"Mel, you can live with us two or three months," Luis all but begged of me.

"I can't," I said, unable to look him in the eye. "I can't."

Deep within I wanted nothing more than to be with him, but I was scared. I gave myself permission to be scared of living in big, bad Cuba. If I had been honest with myself back then, I would have also admitted that I was scared to jump into that real kind of commitment. It was OK to love him, but to be with him, there, was another thing altogether. My brain and my heart were at war.

The mood changed drastically my last twenty-four hours and the morning I was to leave, Luis would barely look my way. I tried to keep my mind on the task at hand—packing. Tears rolled down my face and dropped like bullets on my bag.

The drive to the airport was tense. We could barely get through a sentence without arguing. As we wound into an entrance of the airport and realized we were at the wrong terminal, Luis exploded as his fist slammed the dash. But we both knew none of this was about the airport or the terminal. We were being torn apart and I was the reason.

As I walked through immigration and waved good-bye, Luis's head stayed down, his hand up in a send-off. Tears spilled, running the length of my cheeks, and I waited for him to look up, but he didn't. Finally, I closed the door and turned to go through the security checkpoint, broken.

A week after I returned to Savannah, President Bush announced from Miami that there would be tighter travel restrictions to Cuba. Accusations were made that Castro was developing biological weapons, which the Cuban government vehemently denied.

Cuban-Americans applauded Bush's efforts. My stomach tightened.

Chapter 23

Budapest

April 2, 2002

Two weeks later I sat in the Atlanta airport, waiting for a flight to Paris. Seven hours later, another to Budapest. I physically ached for Luis, yet there I was, about to go on a plane, taking me farther away from him. What was I doing? From a logical point of view, it made no sense at all.

I had spoken to Luis the previous night. He called me to say he couldn't sleep. He wanted to hear my voice. As I listened to his, my throat quivered. Again, he gave his best shot. He didn't want to push, but offered Cuba as an alternative to Hungary for just a couple of months.

I threw in my family. They weren't ready, I said. My dad would not sleep at night. When he went silent, I tried to make him understand this last ode to my mother. I had a one-way ticket with no plans of any kind. But I said that I would come see him very soon.

My brain made its case for my independence and freedom, whatever that even means. As I hung up the phone, I felt sick.

Before my mother died, she became open to the practice of reiki, at the suggestion of her friend, Bobby, who had become a master of the Japanese form of natural healing. From afar, Bobby focused all of his positive energy on my mom, passing his "life force energy" to her, to promote her healing.

"I love you, I love you, I love you," I repeated in my head, as if the words would free themselves and fly to Luis. As if my life force energy would escape to find and lift him when I didn't have the courage to do what I really wanted to do, which was to be with him.

I knew that Luis was my future. Yet, I hid in my fear, packed in a suitcase headed for Eastern Europe, behind the veil of my mother's memory.

The next morning, I pushed myself out the door. In the walls of my self-made steel vault, I told myself that I knew what I was doing, that I was in control of my own path and that I would find my way back to Luis when the time was right.

April 3, 2002

Before takeoff, I sat slightly at an incline, trying to drown out my thoughts of Luis, my mom, and the most unfortunate body odor punctuating my space. I was happy to be in a two-seater aisle, not in between four strangers in the longer rows, but I struggled with my new neighbor who was in dire need of good deodorant.

Eventually the young man fell asleep and snored lightly next to me. I turned on my overhead light and tried to concentrate on Hungarian phrases listed in a book I had bought a couple days earlier. "*Szia*" is hello and "*hello*" is good-bye.

Megszentségteleníthetetlenségeskedéseitekért was listed as an actual word, or rather a string of suffixes fastened to one another. Also, *Legeslegmegszentségteleníttethetetlenebbiteknek* and *Töredezettségmentesítőtleníttethetetlenségtelenítőtlenkedhetnétek.*

Most native speakers wouldn't recognize these words, the book noted, but still, this was by far the most difficult language I had ever attempted. I don't speak French, but even in Paris, by myself for three days, I was able to wing it. Hungarian, I wasn't so sure.

I read more about Budapest, the "Paris of the East," its right-banked residential sectors, Buda and Óbuda, and the artistic left-banked Pest, which is also the commercial core of the city. Other chapters praised the country's classical musical dominance throughout the ages and a burgeoning theater scene. My internal dialogue was one of persuasion, as I tried to convince myself I was going to enjoy my newest adventure.

My eyes grew heavy and I reached overhead to switch off the light. Restless, I imagined pillows of fluff just outside my window, but questions punctured peaceful thoughts: Why was I pushing myself toward more unknown? Did I think I was going to restore what I had lost in the streets of Budapest, following a hollow promise to my mom?

I wanted to believe that maybe my mom could guide me from afar. Maybe she could help me find me again, in the notes of the famed opera houses or the walls of some crazy hostel that I was destined to stay in during my first weeks there.

Chapter 24

A Mismatched LEGO Piece

Upon arrival in Pest, I was on my own. A friend of my father's had very generously offered his apartment to me for a few weeks until I was situated, but with some of his other friends using the space when I arrived, I would have to find my own digs the first two weeks there. Minutes before the plane landed, I scoured the travel book for a decent hostel or hotel. I got off the plane and made my way down the corridors to baggage claim. I did feel a hint of excitement about being in a new country, but my body was in a state of havoc after almost two full days of travel.

I saw my obnoxiously oversize green backpack on the belt and popped it off with a heavy jerk. On nearly forty hours of no sleep, hoisting all that weight onto my back was not as easy as it had been in Savannah. *Hu-umph!* The pack had two metal bars with extra storage space that extended above my head. Why did I bring all this stuff? The truth was I didn't know how long I would stay and I had both summer and winter clothes, with all variants of shoes and boots, casual and spiked, for any occasion. This was totally stupid because I'd probably wear the same five things over and over. But I knew from the airplane report that on this particular day it was still cold and I put on my heavy coat, which made the pack pinch even more.

I walked toward the exit to an ATM. I extracted some amount of Hungarian currency—the forint—and around the corner at a kiosk, requested an international calling card from the saleswoman. A circular booth of telephones was just behind me and as I turned I almost took out another traveler with my backpack. "Oh, I'm so sorry, so sorry," I said, putting my hands out as if to take it back. He waved it off and said something to me in some language I couldn't identify.

I looked up to see two Hungarian security men laughing at me. I'm sure I was a sight to see. They said something to each other and turned and laughed at me again.

F off, I thought, and dropped the bag on the ground. I pulled a ripped page from my pocket and began calling hostels to see if any one of them had an available bed. The first two numbers didn't work, but the third, Backpack Guesthouse, had room. In English, the man politely invited me to stay at the hostel and suggested a shuttle service I could find just outside the airport.

I thanked him and looked down at the monstrosity on the floor. Not able to muster the energy to throw it over my shoulder and onto my back, I grabbed the top loop and dragged the corpse outside. Thankfully, the shuttle came quickly and I gladly handed my pack to the driver just before ducking in and crawling to the second row of seats. The drive through the old, European city was gray and I felt uneasy, like I was riding a motorcycle with no helmet.

At the guesthouse, the front-facing wall resembled a gigantic tie-dyed shirt and was strangely alluring, like those Bugs Bunny swirling eyes that I used to watch on TV as a kid. I paid for a week in advance at the front desk and gingerly walked down a narrow set of stairs behind George, the man I spoke to on the phone. He carried my bag, never once complaining of its deadly weight.

I was introduced to a room no larger than mine in New York, with four mattresses like mismatched LEGO pieces lining the walls. After shoving my bag into a gym-style locker in the room and securing it with a padlock, I was given a tour of the grounds. Each room upstairs was for common use and was painted in other various trippy decor. Bob Marley smiled at me in one room, and a colorful aquarium greeted me in another. All were loaded with pictures of excited and goofy-looking visitors from around the world.

I didn't know why in the hell I was there.

Chapter 25

Lost Along the Danube

I had been in Budapest for a couple of days already. Typically, this would be a happy time for me, walking new streets, looking for unannounced adventures, and sorting out new words and expressions with locals. Yet, I moped. I missed Luis terribly. I thought about him constantly, obsessively.

The day after I landed, I called him to let him know I had arrived safely, but speaking to him was very difficult. He missed me desperately. I missed him, too, I told him, holding back tears. Then he sang a line of "La Flaca" by Jarabe de Palo to me, as he had done in Cuba, and I winced, hearing gravel and hurt in his uneven and lovely tone.

He said I would never know how hard it was for him. He didn't have to say he felt left behind. I knew. I told him I would be with him soon and that I would call again the next day. I hung up, feeling as if someone had died. My eyes swelled; my whole body became heavy. I was so far away from him. What had I done? Why had I run from him? The independence that I clung to felt like an anchor, pinning me to the ocean's floor.

Drained, I mulled around the city for hours and then sat in the corner booth of a café for some time, staring at nothing. I drilled myself: Why was I really here? What was I so afraid of? Why had I run from Luis? Unable to answer those very questions, I couldn't bear to go back to the hostel with swarms of strangers in such close proximity so, for some time, I wandered aimlessly.

Though I knew I wanted to be with Luis long-term, I was used to, even proud of, being independent. I thought I had the strength to separate my emotional attachment to Luis from my "new and exciting" experience.

Later that day, when I called Becky from a pay phone on the street, she quickly noted my instability.

"Mel, you don't have to stay," she said. "You can always come home."

"I know, I know," I replied and told her I'd be OK, my voice rattling. The truth was that the thought of returning home again, not being able to manage in another city by myself once again, felt like failure. I didn't want to be in my hometown. I wanted to be doing something larger than myself.

Close by I sat on a park bench, watching people pass. A girl about my age sat down and struck up a conversation. She was Hungarian, but spoke English well. She asked me if I would be interested in teaching conversational English to corporate professionals. The agency where she worked was desperate for native English speakers, especially Americans.

"Sure," I said, and thanked her as she wrote the phone number and address of the agency down for me.

The rest of the day, I tried to make the most of the city. That night, I went to see the Hungarian National Ballet perform at the Magyar Állami Operaház, or the Hungarian State Opera House, in the center of downtown Pest on the tree-lined Andrassy út, with its cafés and outdoor seating. Following the performance, I walked under the small lights that filled the trees at night. I thought only of Luis.

Chapter 26

The Serb

A week later I interviewed with the small, British-run company hired by corporations to teach everyday English.

On the spot, I signed a contract for a twelve-week session during which I would teach bank employees. A congenial woman named Anne was my direct manager and knew that I would go to Cuba for two weeks in June.

With no formal agenda to follow, I was to begin teaching two times a week the following Tuesday at Citibank, which sat high in the Pest district. Anne guided me through various lesson plans and suggested that I choose two to three exercises to work through per class.

I was a bit nervous because I didn't have formal teaching experience.

That day I was tired and took a tram back to my room to rest. As I approached the staircase, I saw George, who had first helped me at the hostel, smoking one of his many daily cigarettes. Through our brief bits of conversations in the hostel, I learned that he was Serbian. I guessed he was in his mid-thirties. George's energy was unusual, if not oddly charming, and his features were off-putting: a bulbous, pink nose dominated his face and dark, small eyes were unevenly balanced by ratty facial hair that covered his top lip. His mouth seemed to be in a permanent state of pucker. At night, I imagined, he dreamed of lemons.

Appropriately, his humor was acerbic, and as a man of few words, I sensed that he only shared his humor with those who would fully appreciate it.

As I climbed the stairs, I stopped in front of him to say hello. He took a deep drag of his cigarette and flicked into the ashtray sitting on top of the railing.

In his peculiar, small, Eastern European-Truman Capotesque voice, he accused me of being a spy. I laughed and asked why. Because of the tweed trench coat and matching hat that I wore, he said. He teased me about being a femme fatale in an American novel. He was flirting. However, in the end, he said he knew that I couldn't be a spy because he could hear my shoes from a mile away.

We talked about my job interview that day with an English language school and I mentioned that I would go see about a journalist's position with a local English newspaper the following week.

"You're a journalist?" he asked.

"Yes."

"I was a journalist once."

"Where? Here?"

His lemony lips tightened. "No."

"In Serbia?" I asked.

He nodded yes and putted his cigarette out in the ashtray.

"Why don't you write now?"

"I gave it up," he said as he crossed his arms and leaned back on the staircase. "I don't even respond to emails anymore."

I looked at him, puzzled; he eclipsed my next question.

"I stupidly made the switch from sports to politics."

"And they didn't like what you were writing?"

"No."

"Did they want you to stop?"

"They wanted to shoot me."

I had never heard anyone say such a thing.

"Why?"

"Because I wrote what I saw."

I was a little nervous to ponder the subject, but he read my inquisitive eyes.

"I was a war reporter."

I didn't know what to say so I remained silent and let him continue the conversation as he saw fit. He volunteered that although relative peace had resumed in his country, the chaos and terror would rise again. Over 90 percent of those in office were part of Milosevic's old crew. It was simply a matter of time.

"It's really sad," he said. "We used to be happy and then one day everything was taken away. No one can do anything. I tried to do something, but . . ." he shrugged and his words trailed off with no real ending.

Eerily like the conversation I had with the old man in Havana, who sat in a rocking chair and mourned the loss of his country, I only thought that Luis and this shy intellect from Serbia shared experiences that I could never fully understand.

And I, the American, who thought she was worldly because she had traveled to a few countries, didn't really know much about anything.

Chapter 27

Breathe, Mel, Breathe

A daily routine began to form. Every morning I emailed Luis from either the hostel's one computer or a local café, with our back-and-forth writings full of angst and desperation. My trip planned in mid-June couldn't come soon enough.

The rest of the time was spent teaching or visiting the city's sights with Amy, an English actress who was studying opera for the summer. We met at the hostel and became fast friends. With her, I forced myself to fill the days in productive ways. We consulted our books and the city's subway map, getting off at local stops and riding the Danube, with my natural sense of curiosity set on low. Nothing inspired me. Nothing excited me, except for the idea of seeing Luis again soon. I knew I had found completeness in a man, yet was too chickenshit to be with him.

I found it hard to breathe.

Chapter 28

Lost in Translation

May 13, 2002

No email from Luis. With Internet off-limits to Cubans, Luis slipped a dollar bill to a guy at an office daily so that he could write to me. It was an expensive habit, but one he saw to loyally. It was unusual that he had not written.

May 14, 2002

Jimmy Carter spoke to Cubans on live TV from the University of Havana. He was the first American president, past or present, to visit Cuba in forty years. The previous week he had met with Castro to press for human rights and democratic reform while simultaneously asking Bush to end the embargo. News media reports unanimously deemed the effort a failure, though well-intended.

I wanted to beat my fists on the wall, scream to the gods, but I knew no one would hear me.

May 15, 2002

Still no email from Luis. Power could have been out in Cuba, I thought, but for two days? Not normal. I began to worry. To my dismay, I had already set up an appointment that morning to meet an actor looking for an English teacher.

We met at Eckermann Café on Andrassy and discussed his background in theater, followed by a tour of the neighborhood, which he called "Little Broadway." Yet, I couldn't focus, as my mind consistently retreated to Luis. Finally, I was able to excuse myself in a polite way and raced back to an Internet café nearby where I had become a regular.

There I found a string of emails from Luis, short and lovely.

One-liners, they read: *Estoy enomorado de ti.* I am in love with you.

Te extraño. I miss you.

Te necesito. I need you.

In an instant I was relieved. And then sad. *What am I doing here? Why am I not with him?*

A fourth email appeared, strikingly different in tone from the others. He wrote that he wanted to marry me, to have children with me, but how could we when we didn't see each other but every two months?

I started to shake. In an instant, I slammed into that horrible, frightening place that I had worked so hard to stay away from. This was scary, dead Mom territory. I wanted to throw up.

He wrote that he didn't want our relationship to turn *enferma*, which I translated literally to mean sick or bad. Tears dropped hard as I read in circles. I couldn't get past that word, *enferma*. I thought he was writing script about why we weren't going to make it.

And there it was, swift and brutal. I was finally forced to recognize what I didn't want to: I kept moving so not to feel. I ran and I ran, from New York, from Savannah, from the therapist, and finally, from Luis. All I was really doing was running from me.

There was terror in standing still.

My life's shift had been seismic. I had lost, but I also had gained.

I knew what I needed to do. Go home. Be near Luis and stake a real future. It was my first clear thought in two years. With newfound clarity, it was even more difficult to read Luis's words. Beyond his concerns, he missed me; he needed to hear my voice. With blurred vision, I collected my things and scurried to the street in search of a phone card substantial enough to talk to Luis for ten minutes.

Afterward, it was a near run to my apartment, which I had moved into a couple of weeks prior. It was only five in the morning in Cuba, but I didn't care. I had to talk to him. He picked up the phone, groggy. I said I was sorry for calling so early, but I had to teach and I couldn't wait to talk to him until late afternoon.

"How are you?" he asked sleepily.

"I'm not OK," sobbing uncontrollably. I sputtered: "I got your email. What did you mean by *enferma*? What are you saying?"

More sobbing and drooling ensued, followed by me essentially asking the same question to different degrees. Luis tried to break in several times, but I cut him off with more groveling and pleading. All around, it was pretty unpleasant and pitiful. Finally, he squeezed in: "*No te preocupes, Mel, no te preocupes.*"

Don't worry, don't worry, he said, calmly.

"*Cómo?*" I sputtered. "How can I not worry? I just want to leave Hungary and go home. I want to be close to you."

"I need you, too, Mel. It's OK."

I collected myself enough to speak in full sentences.

"Then why did you say that our relationship is becoming *enferma*?'"

He explained that he was scared this was becoming an obsession, instead of a real, palatable relationship. That it was making him crazy being separated.

"Me too," I said, defeated. "Me too."

Luis reassured me that he wanted to be with me, above and beyond anything else. He reminded me that I would be in Cuba in just a couple of weeks and then he started to sing to me again.

I hung up exhausted, but less erratic. In the afternoon Luis's sister, Anabel, called me from Italy with reassuring words and asked me not to try not to overanalyze anything. By then, I was calm and clear. I told her that if she could get Luis to Italy, then I would marry him. I wasn't thinking about a big, white dress. In my mind this was a strategic move to get Luis out of the country. From there we could start a life together somewhere. Anywhere. I even spent some time online looking for teaching posts in Havana, but it quickly became clear that it would be like scaling the Great Wall of China on a winter's day.

Just nineteen days to Luis.

Chapter 29

Wings of an Angel

When I called the next day Luis told me that Luisito was going to be in Cuba for several weeks. This would be their first visit together since he'd left almost a year earlier. I was excited and nervous to meet the little guy. Pictures I'd seen in Luis's house showed a sweet face, though much lighter in tone than either of his parents. His hair was dark blond and his skin appeared to almost resemble mine, minus the freckles. Yet he shared his dad's intense brown eyes and eyebrows that looked unusually wise for a small boy.

For the first time in my life, I felt intimidated by a four-year-old. Luis had never introduced any of his girlfriends to his son. What if he didn't like me? What if he became jealous? I certainly wasn't going to compete with him.

As I sat at the computer writing to Luis about my insecurities, I suddenly wilted, wanting only to go to sleep. It was such a strange reaction because I'm usually a people person. But this was something that had happened since my mother had died. The teensiest whiff of vulnerability on my end set off a series of reactions in me beyond my control, leaving me debilitated. It didn't take much at all, in fact, to set off this reaction.

Just days before, my new friend Amy and I had watched an exceptional performance of *Madame Butterfly* at the Opera House. I was into the music and the incredible beauty of the building when out of nowhere my eyes welled, the intimacy of the setting suddenly too much to absorb. In an instant the darkness carried me somewhere I didn't want to go.

I looked to my left, several rows in front of us, and there was an elderly man asleep, his blue coat blanketing his torso. His mouth was in a perfect oval and there was Mom, sick in her hospice bed, her mouth in a long O. She was a mummy, petrified wood, and the only sign of life was a gurgle and deep gasping for air.

I was back in Manhattan on January 9, 2001.

I was in my apartment when Leanne, my stepsister, called to let me know that the doctors had given my mom two weeks to live. There was nothing more they could do beyond managing the pain.

Mom asked her if Walter and I knew, but she never told us herself that she was going to die. Leanne instead took the charge and called me herself.

"OK," I murmured disoriented, unwilling to organize the words she had just said to me. If I didn't put them in sequential order, maybe they wouldn't be true? She suggested I take a leave of absence from work.

"OK. I'll call you tomorrow and let you know when I'll be there."

I hung up the phone and started to shake uncontrollably. There was an actual earthquake inside me. I was sobbing so hard that drool started to form chandeliers that hung disparately from the sides of my mouth. It hurt so much that I was holding myself in an L position and I couldn't get the cries out that were cutting me in half. I don't remember much else that night, only Jacque, Allison, and Susan, another of my dearest friends from high school and a close confidante to my mom, huddled around me in a tepee of support.

The next morning I went to work around seven or so, and no one was there, except for Margaret. She cried with me and told me that she was proud of me for making the decision to go.

I tried to tie up a few loose ends, breaking down every few minutes to sit like a folded bag in the bathroom. Helping no one by being there, I got my things together, turned my computer off, and discreetly headed for the door. The walls caved in when Farley, who sat across from me, came over to me to hug me. I started sobbing, almost convulsing, and he helped me out the door. I felt numb, and needles jabbed me from the inside out. Walking on the concrete hurt.

I called Leanne and told her what train I would take and that I would pick up Mom's birthday cake. She would turn fifty-three the next day. I walked the long West Side blocks to a boutique grocery store with vibrant fruits and vegetables and ornate bakery. I ordered a small, round cake with cursive, pink letters: HAPPY BIRTHDAY, MARTI.

Loaded down, I took a cab to the train station. The ride to Jersey was flooded with tears. Vague memories of Leanne cooking cranberry chicken and wild rice, the cake being brought out to Mom while we sang "Happy Birthday," are still part of my consciousness, but many of the in-betweens are lost. Yet, Mom's last ode, out of tune with her family's crackly voices, while she sat upright on her hospital bed in the middle of the living room, was just about to send me to my breaking point.

Mom said it was the best birthday she'd ever had. Of course as we all knew it was her last, I thought. We weren't only celebrating her birthday, but her entire life. She opened gifts, handling the elegant wrapping paper more delicately than she ever had before.

It was then that the devil took over. He put his hand out—I didn't want it—but he latched himself to me. If we all knew she was going to die, why did we buy pajamas she'd never wear? He was laughing at me. Why did we purchase makeup she would never use and books she would never read? Why were we celebrating a life that was about to leave us? Why? Why? Why? Stop! Stop! Stop! My insides screamed.

I was drowning in guilt for such vile thoughts, but still, they fired at me. Why were we all putting on our happiest faces when we were all buried in our own terrifying notions of life without my mom? I was furious. Everything was a lie. Here we were singing to Mom, who was no longer vying for life, but succumbing to death. I was struggling to breathe and to place myself in a world without her.

I bathed her for the first time that night. Her stomach was swollen, as if she were eight months pregnant. Her belly button was shut, her ankles full of fluid, three-hundred-pound weights attached to bird legs, knobby knees. Her clavicle pushed bone out and her breasts hung limp, just skin hanging on. Her whole body was tinted a deep, jaundiced yellow. I focused on her face, which winced from the shower water's pressure.

I got her out quickly and then called to Walter, who carried her back to bed. Lee had set out one of her birthday presents—pink pajamas with three butterflies on the front. With difficulty, we got her into them and slowly lowered her back onto the bed.

Jim walked in. "Looking hot in your new jammies," he told Mom, gently touching her hair.

Big, wide eyes met his. "Are you being facetious?"

"No, no, not at all."

"Mom, you look beautiful," I said.

She faded to sleep.

The next day she turned the corner, without asking any of us for permission. No place for words, the next few days and nights were filled with haunting, rhythmic chanting.

The hospice nurse who came in and out of the house at least once a day told us that we all come into the world making noise so there's a pretty good chance we'd leave it doing the same. But those cries, they were deep, not human. No mortal could make those sounds. They launched a formal war with my psyche, corroding any trace of innocence left inside me. They blanketed my nights. I tried to rest on the couch in the living room, just feet from her bed, but the moans streaked through the dark like electrical nodes suctioned to my skin.

Hell, it seemed, had found its way to Morristown.

Once proud to be her source of comfort at the hospital or entertainment while bored at home, I had now been devoured by my devotion to her. She held on to me in the end the way I had to her as an infant.

Compartments in my brain began to fail me. I couldn't focus. My mother's regimen of medicines looked like notebooks of Chinese manuscripts to me. Lee took over Mom's daily pill dosage while I could only manage to crawl in bed with her during light hours. I held her hand, played with her hair, and read letters that came in from friends and family who had just learned of the seriousness of her illness. She had become the master of disguising how sick she really was.

At some point I called Becky.

"I can't do this anymore. I can't watch her like this," I sobbed incoherently. "It's too much for her to take. It's too much for me to take."

She cried with me. "It's OK, Mel, it's OK," she repeated again and again. "You're not a bad person. You just need peace."

She was right, I did need peace, but to consider the equation minus Mom was anything but peaceful.

The next day I got an email from Susan.

From: Susan Main
To: Melanie Bowden
Date: Wed, 17 Jan 2001
Melanie-

I feel an urgency to write things down. I want your mom to know so many things that I feel about her, and I know a lot of other people do too.

I want you to know how much knowing your mom has changed me—really changed me. She taught me to sacrifice for others, but to not sacrifice myself. She taught me to always find the humor in life. She taught me to honor the artist in me. She taught me courage—that I have the power to change my circumstances. She taught me to always work hard for those you love. She taught me to be accepting of all people.

But most of all, I think her greatest achievement is you. She has raised a woman who is confident, and wise, and joyful and talented. She has raised someone who teaches me as much as she did, if not more.

You are the best friend I have ever known. I love you so much—fiercely! I am sending my love, energy, and support through these wires. I am there for you—we all are! And I pledge to not leave you when you need me the most. I'll be there to bug you—even when you want to be left alone!

I love you, I love you, I love you.
Susan

I responded:

From: Melanie Bowden
Sent: Thurs, 18 Jan 2001
Subject: Re:
Thank you, sweet Sue.

Beautiful note, made me cry. I'll read to Mom in a little while. She has a couple of people visiting her now. They are laughing, telling stories, but I can't seem to go in the room and join them. We laugh some, too, but other times I can't seem to muster up the energy to be polite and gay. They also need their own time with her.

Mom's friend, George, is coming later today. He's going to lose his mind. She looks dead. Her skin is yellow, her mouth hangs open, her teeth even look different. Her breathing is disconnected. No real pattern to it. It's filled with fluid from her lungs. She exhales like she's underwater. I find myself unintentionally breathing with her, pausing with her, wanting to take the breath for her. Sometimes she'll breathe in, it doesn't come out, we all hold our breath with her, she exhales after what seems an eternity, and we go back into the land of waiting. Every night I am amazed, impressed she's made it through another. I tell her repeatedly that it's OK, to let go when she needs to. We've all told her, even Jim, who keeps claiming that he's going to go right behind her.

But I know she hears us. Last night, late, I was holding her hand, talking to her, telling her I love her, and she opened her eyes, twitched her hand. Went back out in thirty seconds, but she heard me, acknowledged me. So I know she'll hear your letter when I read it to her.

I sound like a lunatic, but I just want to run around and tell those I love how much I love them, just in case anything ever happened to me like this. So please know I love you so much, for your spirit, your gigantic heart, your support, always. And for being a total, raving nut. I love it all. Give your family a big kiss for me.

Love, Mel

She responded:

Dear Mellie,

I heard an interesting story in my yoga class last night. The yoga teacher said that Michelangelo carried around a big lump of marble with him. And he knew that God had already created the statue of the angel—his only job was to chip away the excess stone—to liberate the angel within. He didn't MAKE it, it was there all the time, underneath everything. It reminded me of you and your mom—that no matter what happened in your pasts, that bond between you has always been there, underneath everything. And now it's been stripped down to its essence—to its "angel." And that's something you'll always have.

I hope that makes some sense to you. It did to me, but then again, I am a total, raving nut.

I love you, I love you, I love you.

Susan

Mom died the next day. It was around eight at night. Jim, two of Mom's oldest friends, and Leanne and I were in the room with her. My brother and aunt had already gone to rest at her house an hour away. I was holding Mom's hand when she took that last breath in. Its depth gripped us all.

"It's OK to go, Mom," I said, holding her right hand with both of mine, my face resting on hers. Next to meeting my children for the first time, it was the most intimate moment of my life. "Let go. Walter and I will be fine."

Her breath was still in, but her eyes were holding, holding, holding.

I begged of her: "Please let go. It's OK, it's OK. Go. Go."

Her eyes looked at me and then locked. Earth opened right there in front of me, wrapped its arms around Mom, and took her. Her energy, her person, all of those combinations of life and love, marriage and motherhood that make people who they are, slipped. She escaped through a crack, and there was no time to reach out and pull her back. I couldn't breathe.

"Jim! Mom is gone!" I screamed in my head as I fell into him and latched on to his chest. I made a loud sound as I exhaled her unfinished breath onto his sweater.

Eventually, everyone left me in the room alone. I crawled in the narrow hospice bed with her. She looked like my mom, but the sunlight had disappeared. I was left lying next to a beaten and bruised chassis. I concentrated on her hands, which I held with my own, as my head curled, childlike, into the side of her arm. My hands were hers, with precise reflection in the size and shape, down to the fingernails.

After some time, I found the courage to look at her face. The grimace that had dominated for days had faded completely. She was beautiful and peaceful, something that I would have thought impossible. In my mind, the terror of resting beside my dead mother would have been overwhelming, yet there I was with her, flower to flower, wood to wood. Unfrightened. This was nature.

We were organic matter, connected in a way that transcended everyday life. I still held life and she didn't, but I experienced the passing of her life. It was larger, more beautiful even, than anything I could have imagined.

Until then, I thought death would have been passive, an inactive kind of thing. In the everyday language of "so-and-so died in her sleep," I assumed a level of disconnection, as if the actual act of it was quiet and unassuming. But Mom's passing was active, a torrential force that drew us in and then like that, she checked out, but not without connecting with me first.

There is no better way of honoring the person who brought you into the world than to be with her when she leaves it and carry her memory forward.

Lying next to her, I distinctly remember wanting to hug the inside of her. That angel Susan talked about. The outside wasn't my mother anymore. Her body became a casket to her disease, but not her soul. And it was right then that I fully grasped the essence, the real spirit of my mother, more precious than a pretty face or a great sense of humor. I wanted her. The real her. Desperately so.

Chapter 30

You're Talking,
But I Can't Hear You

It was June in Budapest and time for me to return to Cuba. I was having a hard time finding clothes that still fit me, as my girth continued to grow under the weight of daily fills of almás pites, the divine Hungarian combos of apples, sugar, and dough that were available on almost every street corner and called me by name. At a local market, I bought a pair of linen pants with a drawstring tie so I could be comfortable. But I still packed my bikini.

My flight was about nine hours in all from Budapest to Paris, and Paris to Havana. I filled my time with books, magazines, movies, and finally, pacing, but it was too much to stand.

When I arrived I waited very impatiently for my bag and all but ran out to find Luis. This was a different terminal and the rooms were long and wide. I couldn't find him. I looked everywhere, even around large potted plants. Where was he? From behind I was grabbed and hugged and then kissed. He had rather enjoyed my overly expressive concern from afar as I searched for him.

He was with a friend, nicknamed Coco. (His head actually looked like a coconut, with tan-colored fuzz on top and all). Coco drove and Luis sat in the front seat. He slipped his hand in between the two front seats to the back and held mine, our fingers laced like a secret. I wanted him to sit in the back with me, but by then I understood that we might look like a paying tourist couple and that could create problems for Coco. It was uncomfortable, but I had come to accept that's the way things were. Luis looked at me for a long time, neither of us speaking.

When we got back to his apartment, he sat opposite me, our faces only inches apart, and placed his hands on my knees. He asked about Hungary and the minutia that we couldn't talk about over email. I told him about my daily outings with Amy and teaching, which I had discovered was not my calling, but it was hard to concentrate on much else other than Luis.

"You're talking and I can't hear you," he said, repeatedly combing his right hand through my hair and running his thumb along the high point of my cheekbone and the edge of my upper lip. He pressed the fleshy underside of his to mine as two of his fingers played with the tip of my ear and the other set trailed down the back of my head, the fold of my neck, and the length of my spine. He drew me in closer and we were sharing the same breath as he moved a slow and deliberate trail of kisses from my mouth to just above my lip and along the outer edges of my cheeks. The narrow slope of his nose nestled into mine before resuming the languid series of kisses to each of my eyelids and the stretch of my forehead. When he pulled back, the brown of his eyes was marbled with tones of olive, as the late-afternoon sun streamed through his bedroom shutter. "It doesn't seem real that you're here."

I smiled. "I know."

Luis wanted to walk the Malecón, which we did in a limb lock, despite Havana's fierce May afternoon sun. As we moved, I closed my eyes and pressed my nose deep into the crook of his neck. Luis veered left and pulled me into him as his back leaned against the concrete wall. As the sun faded and night rose we fell into each other, unaware of English or Spanish, Savannah or Havana. It was just us on the ocean's sidewalk and the tsunamis of my dreams withered to waves that crashed against the wall where Luis and I sat with no clock demanding our attention.

Chapter 31

Viva La Revolución!

The next morning, in my dream I was in water again. I rode waves in long strides, up and over and down again, with strangers, but peacefully so.

Suddenly, I was jerked from my sleep by the sound of Fidel Castro's voice, which came through our window in short, powerful bursts:

"*Socialismo o muerte!*" he called. "*Socialism or death!*"

My eyes fully opened. I imagined his index finger, nearly fifty years in command, pointed and firm, aimed at the sky, as I had seen him on TV so many times before.

His calls were met with loud chants from the crowds of Cubans: "*Venceremos!*" *We will succeed!*

Then: "*FI-DEL! FI-DEL! FI-DEL!*"

Wrapped up in Luis, who remained unfazed and asleep, I looked at his brown skin. His long eyelashes curled upward as he slept. I freed one of my hands from under his arm and ran my fingers through his hair. I kissed his face, where the side of his nose met the beginnings of his cheek. He stirred, barely opened one eye, and put his ear into the air, taking in the rally outside.

"*Estúpidos,*" he mumbled and fell back asleep.

I rummaged at the base of the bed for a robe and pulled it on me as I banged my way into the hall and then through the bathroom door. The long, rectangular window above the toilet was swiveled open a good three inches, but Fidel had even captured the ocean's attention that day; it wouldn't offer even a hint of breeze. In mid-June, with no air conditioning, the house was an inferno.

I stepped up onto the retired bidet to look out onto Plaza Martí, which sits along the Malecón. Normally, cars would have raced the narrow city track situated between the plaza and the seawall, but that day the streets were filled only with people.

Castro must have been lifted high on the stage in the oblong plaza, though I couldn't see him. My sight was blocked by hundreds of waving red, white, and blue flags and throngs of people lining the streets, as well as soldiers who had infiltrated the battered rooftops of surrounding buildings. If I were a painter, their dark green silhouettes would have become abstracts, laced into laundry wires roping through the sky.

Fidel's voice remained strong and loud, but it was difficult to decipher the echoes of anger. My Spanish language skills were light-years from where I had started, but Cuban dialect, I have learned after many years, is not an easy thing to conquer. Cubans like to snake off the latter half of words.

"They do use the plural form here, don't they?" I once asked Luis.

"Yes, smart-ass," was the only response I received.

I stepped off of the bidet and went back to the bedroom. Just inside the doorway, I paused as Fidel called out:

"*Pioneros por el Comunismo!*" *Pioneers of Communism!*

In unison, only young voices responded: "*Seremos como el Che!*" *We will be like Che!*

This was a far stretch from any pep rally I had ever attended as a kid. These were chants that Luis had memorized as a young boy. Perhaps they registered somewhere in his consciousness as he rolled over and slit an eye open. Luis put his arm where I should have been and I crawled back into place. He roped himself back into me as his caramel eyes sleepily looked up into mine.

"Does this make you nervous?" he asked with a slight nod to the madness outside.

"No," I said. "Not now," as if I were a seasoned professional in communist sport.

I asked Luis what Fidel was going on and on about. He laughed and said that he was on a jaunt about Cuba's Achilles heel—George Bush, Jr. (or Baby Bush, as one of my former bosses used to say). Bush had just added Cuba to Washington's "axis of evil" list of countries, and Fidel, in turn, was pissed.

"And here you are, an American in my bed," Luis said, wrapping his arms around me and pulling me in closely. "*La Americana.*" He smothered me with small kisses all over my face, forcing me to burrow into his chest for safety.

"*La enimiga.*" The enemy.

"Vicious," I returned, as my eyes widened. I laughed at my absurd attempt at terror.

Fidel's voice suddenly amplified, as if someone had cranked up the volume and it sounded slightly as if he were yelling at me, one of only a few Americans on the island. I all but jumped, but not Luis, who was stretched lazily and pulled himself out of bed, heading toward the bathroom. When he came back, he told me that we couldn't go outside for hours.

I had coloring books and pencils for Luisito. Luis grabbed them, brought them to the bed, and started coloring in one of them. I picked up the Mickey Mouse book and penciled my own version of a lion, which I later named Luis the Lion and gave to him.

Outside of Luis's apartment in Havana (*courtesy of Melanie Simón*).

Eventually we roused enough to head downstairs. Ana sat on the sofa smoking a cigarette while she watched the scene below unfold on TV.

"*Mami, por Dios*," said Luis, snapping off the blurry vision.

I learned that there were only two television channels at that time in Cuba and both were running Fidel and the masses. We hung out, sequestered for hours, until finally the rally broke and we were free to roam and gather a handful of things for Luisito and his grandparents.

The next day we again met up with Coco and his wife, to make the trip to Santa Clara. Almost everything about Coco is loud— his movements, his gestures, his tone of voice. Everything about him is overt and a bit wild, so he's not one I would have pegged as a friend of Luis.

They picked us up in their blue car, sans air conditioning on that fryer of an island. Turned out, Coco also likes his music loud. Nothing was particularly shocking about this, but to his credit, for most of the trip, he at least played good Marc Anthony salsa. An hour into the trip, it began to rain hard. There weren't any wind-shield wipers on the car, and my body tightened as Coco contin-ued to drive fast, as if unaware that there was a solid front of water just under our noses. Water began to queue up along the rim of the window to my left and I realized my door wasn't fully shut. I knew it wasn't a matter of pulling it taut. It simply wasn't going to close. Water started coming in faster on my side. I'll admit I was being a bit of a princess, but I didn't want to get wet because I had on a decent pair of pants and top for my new introductions.

With a clenched jaw, I was uncomfortable, but jolted by my built-in censor that reminded me that this was how Cubans lived. I moved my bag from the middle to the window seat and slid into its place.

Luis was in the front passenger seat and began to cuff his right sleeve until it was above his elbow, then rolled down his window and began to use his front arm, a gray towel in hand, as a windshield wiper. At the same time, Coco furiously used a tissue to swipe the inside condensation on the glass. Finally, Coco's wife asked him to pull over. I breathed a sigh of relief as he slowed to a stop under a bridge.

Hyper Coco couldn't handle any more than twenty minutes of refuge before he took off with the same furor as before. Again, I tensed, but remained quiet. At one point, Luis looked back at me and winked. He knew that the human windshield wiper and defrost system routine had me a bit rattled.

Eventually the rain tapered and we stopped at a gas station. It was there that Luis unrolled a cigarette, exposing the tobacco. He got out of the car and smeared the dark brown mass all over the outside glass.

He peered in at me, and I shrugged in question.

"The nicotine sucks up the water," he said, smiling.

Chapter 32

Pi-Chi!

The figure of a small boy stood at the top of the stairs.

"Pi-Chi!" Luis called, his arms open as he skipped every other step until he reached his little one standing in the shadows. He scooped him up, cub-like, and kissed him all over his face.

I stayed at the base of the stairs until Luis looked down and motioned with his head to come up. They disappeared through the doorway, and nerves ping-ponged in my stomach.

Timidly, I walked through the doorway, greeted by many smiling faces, and landed several *besitos* (the small, customary kisses on the cheek) from each family member.

A petite face was buried into Luis's neck and arms wrapped tightly around.

"Papi," said Luis to his little one, who didn't move from his nesting spot.

Luis rubbed his back and again: "Papi, this is Melanie."

His head lifted just slightly, and his large brown eyes briefly moved my way, but he never looked at me directly.

I smiled. "*Hola*," I said.

Nothing back. Conversations among all of the family members resumed. I was in the dark because I couldn't follow any one in particular. I sat quietly, engaged as much as possible without contributing. It was too overwhelming.

Luisito eventually let go of his dad and began playing around the room, but still he wouldn't look my way, much less get near me. He needed time, so I gave it to him.

The following day, we piled into the car, with Luisito seated next to me in the backseat while his dad drove. He sat quietly looking out the window. I wasn't going to interact until he was ready, so again I waited.

A bit down the road, on our way to a nearby lake, young Luis sat up on his knees (car seats are unheard of in Cuba) and leaned into me. He pulled my sunglasses off my head and laughed. Touchdown. He was communicating.

I took miniature frames off him and wriggled the tight fit onto the bridge of my nose. He giggled and slipped my pink ones onto his face. They slid down his nose so he tried again. "Whoop! There they go again!" we roared.

Luis watched from the rearview mirror and joined in the laughter. At ease, Luisito squirmed into the side of me until we reached the lake, giggling most of the way.

There we rented a small boat and took to the water, arriving at the foot of a tall piling of rocks. Luis picked up his son and climbed the flattest of the stones until he reached a small pool above. I followed, settling

Luis and Luisito, Matanzas, Cuba (*courtesy of Melanie Simón*).

on what seemed the steadiest rock, and dipped my toe in water, jerking immediately from the freezing temperature.

I opened my arms to Luisito, who situated himself into my lap before watching his father make a one-eighty and dive into the water.

"You're crazy!" I yelled. "It's freezing!"

Luis's head shot up.

"*Que frío!*" and laughed, swimming as quickly as he could to the other side. There, he and Coco climbed another set of rocks and on count, jumped, both letting out exaggerated hollers on impact.

Howling and giggling with them, the responsibility in the thirty-five pounds of innocence that sat on my legs was large. I knew Luis trusted me with his son.

Chapter 33

The Real Deal

Being together was easy, but living together in the same country was an entirely separate issue. I couldn't find a way in my mind to be in Cuba for any extended period of time that made sense. At the same time, Luis needed to find his way out legally so that he could come back and visit his family, with whom he is so close.

I thought (without knowing any facts about how to do so): I could marry Luis, but that would mean more separation from him as we filed paperwork, a lot of travel on my part (which equaled money that I didn't have), and copious amounts of explaining to everyone at home. The latter made me most nervous.

I didn't want to feel sorry for myself, but I did wonder on occasion why it was so easy for other couples so much of the time. They meet, they fall in love, they marry, they have babies. We met, we fell in love, but the being together in any one place to be married and living as a pair was daunting.

So many of our conversations began with the same hypotheticals: What if Luis could get a visa to a European country and I could meet him there? I could find a job. It could work and my family wouldn't be so worried. But then there was no assurance that he could get a visa, as he had been denied. Maybe I could get permission to study at the university in Cuba and we could be together? But then what? Would we just stay in Cuba? That wasn't going to work.

Sitting in Luis's room, we were plagued by these very questions. "What if . . ." I started and stopped abruptly.

Luis looked at me quizzically as I gnawed my thumbnail.

"What if we got *married*? Like the real thing?"

"Yes. *Yes*. I love you, Mel."

Yes, yes, yes! Suddenly, we were engaged. There was no ring or planning or logical thought behind it.

It was mindboggling, but somehow it made sense. We were ecstatic. I all but jumped and screamed in a fit of joy. Like children we ran downstairs and announced to Ana that we were going to get married. Her excitement must have been met with hesitation, as surely this meant her son and closest friend would move away, but she hid it beautifully and celebrated our happiness.

In a matter of days we decided on December 4 of that year. We would marry in Cuba to begin the formal paperwork and then we could have another service in the States once he joined me at home. A Cuban lawyer and friend of Luis's told us it typically took six to nine months to get a visa.

Luis's grandmother and aunts began calling from all over Cuba to congratulate us. It was totally and completely surreal to me. Crazy, crazy! But Luis and I were so happy.

On the plane ride back to Paris and then Budapest, I was upset after leaving Luis, but so excited about our future that I rode calmly. I was dying to finish out my teaching term, get home, and put on my mother's ring. I told Luis that I wanted to wear her diamond, the classic, gold Tiffany cut that Jim gave to her and she left to me.

I thought about my family, my friends. What would they say? I was going to be a wife! I was going to be a stepmother!

Growing up in the conservatively minded city of Savannah, I had always assumed that I would marry an American with no baggage, meaning no divorces and no children. It was strange to have entered the world in which I found myself wading, but intuition pushed me forward. I didn't care what people thought. Luis and I were in love, and nothing was stronger than that.

Chapter 34

The Elephant in the Room

The day after I returned to Budapest, I was hit hard with something I had picked up in Cuba. I felt like death for about thirty-six hours, but my new roommate, Omer, an Israeli medical student, home-cooked chicken soup for me. I had moved from my palace to a modest but decent rented room in the Pest district. Omer and I became fast friends, and consequently he was always feeding me outrageously good food—homemade falafel, yogurt sauces, and pasta and eggplant dishes with olive oil that his mother sent from Israel. As my mother would have said, all was divine.

Once I was able to pick my head up, I found a nearby Internet café in my new neighborhood. No one in my family yet knew about my engagement and I needed to tell my dad first. He was in the process of moving from one house to another in his new hometown of Vidalia and didn't have a phone hooked up yet. Certainly, I couldn't call him at work. That's not the kind of thing you tell your dad when he's in the midst of running a bank.

But really, *really*, I was chickenshit. I didn't know how to make that call. So I put it into an email. I wrote in the header, "I'm Engaged!"

Looking back, I probably should have buffered that a bit more. His only daughter, twenty-six years old, living in Budapest, Hungary, writes to say that she is marrying a man she's seen four times, who lives on Castro's communist island and doesn't speak English.

I didn't hear from him for three days. I was dying, checking email every few hours of every day. I didn't know what to think. Finally, his message arrived. While he was shocked by the news and apprehension seeped from the pixels of my foreign computer screen, he gave me his blessing and said he hoped that he could meet "this young man very soon." There were questions about how long the process would take, where we would live, and what we would do. I could only answer vaguely, as I didn't know myself. But I would come home soon. I needed roots to start this new journey.

Even if he was unhappy with my choice, my dad still chose support, as did the rest of my family and friends.

I began to call them all. As if they had conferred on the topic, their responses were laced with the same striking sincerity: shock and apprehension but ultimately, congratulations.

After all that I had been through, they all genuinely held my happiness in great regard, but still, in each conversation they tepidly treaded the same waters: Have you really thought about this? Are you sure this is what you want?

What they wouldn't ask, but I knew that each considered: Was I attempting to fill a void with the newness of this relationship? How could this be so soon? I had met Luis only four months after my mom died. And like the skirting around with my father, the big elephant that no one dared to touch: how did I know that he wasn't just marrying me to get out of the country?

Had I been in their shoes I would have asked those very questions. Yet, there was no mixing of the two for me. My mother and

Luis were distinct people with two separate places in my heart. I never felt that Luis was filling the loss of my mother. No one could do that. As for him marrying me to get out of Cuba, it simply wasn't true. I knew this, but there was no way to explain it. They would still doubt until they met him and maybe even then. But I was comfortable in my decision and that would have to be enough.

I knew that it seemed irrational and maybe even irresponsible for me to marry someone from Cuba, and someone so different from me in many ways. Yet, in perspective, nothing was stranger than my mother dying at fifty-three. Sure, my decision to marry Luis didn't make sense on paper, I agreed, but at that point in my life, what did? My mom was gone and I had never imagined I would lose her before I got married and had children.

Chapter 35

Grim Reaper

My dream was agitated. It was a running stream of the same event and coordinates over and over again. My aunt Cathi, my mom's sister, was in a room with me. She was young, maybe a teenager. But then she wasn't really Aunt Cathi. She was my mom, if not in face, then in spirit. In dreams dual citizenship of the same body is allowed, I suppose. The sisters in their unison felt rebellious (much like my aunt was as a young person), with short, bobbed red hair. We were in a cramped upstairs bedroom of someone's house. I felt locked away.

My aunt/mother looked at me and said, "You're going to die soon."

I retorted, "Why do you think that?"

"Because you've got more stomach than people understand."

I knew what she meant in the dream but not when I woke up. "And Walter?"

She brushed the comment off. "Long time."

I said that I wanted to live at least long enough to see my grandchildren. Then a Jack Russell appeared just outside the small bedroom window, scratching and clawing until it squeezed through. Now, Mom, Aunt Cathi, and I were three separate individuals in the room.

Mom said, "Get that dog away from me."

And the sweet little dog suddenly looked vicious, like a canine Grim Reaper, and attempted to fly over me to get at Mom, who, by then, was standing behind me. I reared up and hit it in the nose with a short, thick drinking glass (that appeared out of nowhere). The ferocious dog retracted, slipped away, and suddenly wasn't so frightening.

I woke up. Damn death dog. Wish I could have slammed it with an entire glass building.

Chapter 36

Castro, Bush, and the Racy Tango

I rode out my last few weeks in Budapest lonely, save several days that my friend, Zia, came to visit. He teased me as I curled into my pillow at night with Luis's scented shirt. I missed him desperately and I began to miss home. Home was closer to Luis, although not much given my restrictions as an American.

I received an email from Luis that first week of July. He was worried that Fidel was going to shut down the US consulate. The word around Cuba was that Bush was going to send two large ships to the coast of Cuba and anyone who wanted to come to the US could. This was following an announcement by Castro that, according to a recent poll, more than 70 percent of the Cuban population supported his version of socialism. So Bush, in his best mine's-bigger-than-yours bluff, called him out on it.

Those two were dancing a racy tango, one behind the other, and Luis and I were very concerned. The Bush-Castro rift was gaining strength and it seemed enough to damage all relations between the two countries. If they cut off all ties, where would that leave us?

It was stressful, but we couldn't focus on it. All we could do was go ahead as planned. I couldn't do anything anyway until I got home.

In Savannah, my father had quietly put his own wheels in motion. He made a call to a lawyer, who made a call to a friend, who made a call to another friend who knew someone in Miami. The latter was a Cuban woman, a consultant for people just like me, looking for help to get someone out of Cuba.

Her fee was acceptable. She told me that if we married in Cuba and then filed papers, it could take a year or more to get Luis out of there. If we applied for a K-1, or fiancé visa, for Luis through the US government, then it should only take about three months. This was music to my ears.

Once in the US, he and I would have to marry within three months of his arrival. *I'd marry him at airport baggage claim*, I thought, *if I could get him to Savannah*. To apply I needed documentation for him—birth certificate, photos, the works, as well as three years of my income taxes, a note from the bank as to how much money I had, and bios about each of us. In addition, I had to send copies of two plane tickets to Cuba and two photos of us together.

Here's where it became a little tricky. The trips I had already taken to Cuba were without a US-backed license to do so. The consultant didn't think that this would be a point of contention, as she didn't believe the US government was going to give me a hard time about my reasons for being there. I only needed to prove that Luis and I had actually met and shared some time together. In other words, I wasn't a hired bride.

But because this was a new life for us, we didn't want any chance for mishaps. We needed to find the patience to do things correctly. Therefore, I would have to make two more trips with formal permission. This would take more money and more time. The idea of a December wedding was out the door.

At the top of my list were finding a job and the means to get to Cuba with a visa. The first was easy. I returned to my old restaurant job. This was not what I wanted to do, but I would have some flexibility with travel as I could usually find someone to pick up shifts.

As for the visa, I found an organization in the Midwest that fostered direct assistance to Cubans living with AIDS in Havana. The purchase of an individual license under the auspices of their general license would allow me to be in Cuba for up to two weeks. The only requirement was that I deliver a box of medical supplies or donate cash to a church in Central Havana.

I booked my ticket to Cuba for September, thrilled not only to see Luis (it would be two and a half months apart by the time I got there), but also happy to be out of the US on the first anniversary of 9/11, which was overwhelming to me.

In the weeks before my trip I collected various samples from doctors and dentists I knew around town. Generously, they all loaded bags of toothpaste and brushes, floss and rinse, as well as bandages, aspirin, antacids, and the like. All equally fascinated, they asked much about Cuba, its conditions, and the people. They wanted to know what would happen once Castro was gone one day. All I could offer were personal observations, nothing more. I was still a novice at Cuban culture and life.

Come September, on the flight to Miami, I flipped through the in-flight magazine in record time and pursed my lips while knocking my knees back and forth. I had to spend the night in Miami and then return to the airport the next morning. The charter company requested that I arrive three hours before the flight. Thank God I got there even earlier.

Finding the terminal was a challenge, as no one in the airport knew where it was. It was like some guarded secret and finally, one official was finally able to direct me.

Among the others waiting, a handful of Cubans were old-school elegant, quietly sitting in their tailored shirts, fitted pants, and Italian shoes. Their watches were expensive, but tasteful. Pacing the floor were the "Miamified" young guys, decorated with gold, and lots of it. It was an all-out show of necklaces, watches, earrings, and bracelets and the more audacious, the better.

Other seats and stances were taken by the *guajiros* (country folks) of Cuba, who, in their own way, tried to one-up each other with their gargantuan cowboy hats and belt buckle bling. Finally, I, the *gringita*, in all her paleness, stood with the others in the first of four lines. One line was to check visas, licenses, and passports, one was to search and weigh luggage, the third was to pay taxes on the overweight baggage, and finally the last was check-in. It was absolute inefficiency at its best.

This was identical to what I had experienced in Budapest when I was asked to pay for two separate items at two separate registers that shared the same countertop. Communism is exhausting.

Though the pre-boarding process was long, the flight was not. Thirty-five minutes on a small Gulfstream and I was reminded of how close we were, though seemingly moons apart.

I crossed passport control easily, with only a few noted remarks about my visa and visit to the church. My box of supplies was met with relative ease and it appeared no one had the patience to pull each individual item for inspection. I had been cleared to leave when a female guard on my left at the exit put her hand out. I stopped. She flagged the other guard to my right and nodded to my purse, a *New York Times* overflowing from the top.

"*El periódico?*"

My jaw clenched. *Don't take my* New York Times. *Don't take my* New York Times.

"*No, pasa, pasa,*" the woman said and waved me on.

It was the helpless thing that got me. There was nothing I could say or do at the mercy of two guards who may, or may not, be having a good day.

As I walked out into the steamy, overcast heat, my anger was lost in an instant when I saw Luis on the other side of the gate. I smiled widely, pushed my way out of the crowd, and jumped to Luis.

"Oh, I missed you," I released in a deep exhale.

His sunglasses were on, but pushed up and resting over his eyebrows, and I kissed him all over his face and neck.

"Me too, Mel," Luis said, as we met in the middle for a big smooch on the lips.

At Luis's home I was beginning to feel more comfortable. I could communicate more with Ana, as well as their family and friends who popped in from time to time.

The back garden at the Hotel Nacional where I again sat while Luis worked one day on, one day off, had become more than a space. It had taken on a personality, speckled with guinea and parakeets snuggled into a small tree on the lawn, shaded by two straw hats, their strings tied to make an umbrella. The birds looked content and so was I. Completely detached from any existence in the capitalist world, I wrote and I read as a gringo couple, more alabaster than I, with overly sunburned shoulders and noses, jumped at the sound of bongos in the corner. The middle-aged pair, stiff as boards, made me smile with each awkward step.

Chapter 37

Santo

A na invited us one evening to go to a *fiesta*. Luis returned
from work, tired and tense, following twelve hours of hot
sun and diesel, which never produced enough money. He took a
quick shower and descended the stairs, crisply clean and smelling
of Issey Miyake cologne, a gift brought from Italy by Anabel.

We hopped in the car, off to the house of Ana's *santo*, or *padrino*,
who is a priest of Santería, an Afro-Cuban religion that grew from
the slave trade. For many years teachings were only passed by word
of mouth, but today literature does exist for priests who focus on
the core of Santería, which is to bond human beings with powerful, but mortal spirits called orishas. An orisha is a representation
of Olodumare (God) and followers believe that the orishas will
aid them in life if they celebrate associated rituals through dancing, speaking, singing, drumming, and eating with the spirits. In a
mutually beneficial relationship, the orishas will only continue to
exist with the presence of loyal worshippers.

Santería priests can be male and female and go through intense
training of various sorts, but much is dedicated to learning both
traditional medicine and herbalism, as they will become valued
nutritional and spiritual advisors to Cubans. Following, there is an

initiation, in which a priest is "reborn into a spirit," making the commitment to serve one of the orishas. With this comes "special powers," including the ability to predict the future. Divination is determined by the way in which a set of palm nuts or coconuts break and fall at the throw of a priest's hand.

When slaves from the Yoruba tribe of West Africa, what is now Nigeria, landed in Cuba, they were not able to practice indigenous customs, including religion. For survival, they hid their orishas behind Catholicism, dressing them as saints. Santa Barbara veiled Changó, who embodies justice and strength and is associated with lightning and fire. Saint Lazarus disguised Babalú-Ayé, a caregiver to the sick. Ana's orisha, Ochún, is the Yoruba goddess of the river, but long masqueraded as Our Lady of Charity. Sensual and sensitive, Ochún is represented by water, dance, the color yellow, sweets, and money, among other things.

Similar to that of the US, African culture in Cuba was suppressed for many years and it wasn't until the 1920s and '30s that African-Cuban culture, or Afro-Cubanism, was celebrated openly in any sort of way. When Castro came into power in 1959, he extended opportunities for education, health care, and artistic expression to all on the island, but religions of every kind were pronounced dead on the spot.

Castro himself had been educated by the most prodigious of Catholics, the Jesuits, but declared Cuba an atheist state as he took the reigns as the country's fledgling president. Christmas trees, rosaries, the observance of Shabbat, and offerings to *santos* disappeared from plain sight. There wasn't direct persecution for worship, but participating in religious services would exclude citizens from membership in the Communist party. Without the government affiliation there was no access to jobs or many of the social services suddenly available to all citizens, regardless of color or status.

In context, the lack of religion wasn't an entirely horrible and radical ideal to everyone. Castro's predecessor, Fulgencio Batista, a one-time moderate who became dictator following his own coup d'etat in 1952, had grossly mistreated and misrepresented most of the country, catering only to the upper classes. Batista had encouraged the construction of casinos with the promise of government backing and American mobster Meyer Lansky led the charge. Gambling, corruption, and police brutality ruled the island. Unhappy citizens began leaning toward the revolution that was occurring in Cuba's countryside, as Fidel, his brother, Raúl, and Che Guevara pushed through, promising equality to all people.

As Batista fled the country on January 1, 1959, Castro's leadership was a sign of hope for many on the island. There were those who saw the bar on religion simply as a shift of the new movement and jumped onboard with the Marxist-Leninist bundle, but others who wished to preserve traditions in worship were forced to move underground for the next forty years.

It was only in the back, windowless rooms of residences across Cuba that quiet exchanges of small gifts continued each year on January 6, the important Catholic calendar holiday *El Día de Los Reyes*, or the Day of Three Kings. Santería ceremonies, held to bring orishas together with followers, held an advantage during the tenuous times, Luis told me, because they can be carried out in the private homes of its priests, who fit their humble settings with altars.

In 1992 Cuba dropped atheism from its constitution and in December of 1997 reinstated Christmas as an official holiday, just weeks before a visit by Pope John Paul II. He was the first pontiff to go to the Communist Caribbean island and hundreds of thousands of Cubans rallied for the papal mass. On its heels, a new Cuban paradigm based in Santería crawled from hiding and out into the open with celebrations that reflect a symbiotic relationship with Catholicism. Many Cubans, like Ana, today consider themselves practitioners of both religions and embrace integrated symbols, like the use of holy water and saintly figurines during the African ceremonies.

Mind you, I knew zip about any of this when I stepped into the front parlor of the small house, full of people, with Ana and Luis on that particular evening. A bowl of water, pink rose petals floating in its bath, sat just inside at the base of the door. Ana dipped her hands in and rubbed them together. I silently studied all as Luis took my hand, waiting patiently to pass through the crowd.

A makeshift altar sat directly in front of us at the back of the room. My view was limited by the comings and goings of others, an intricate, moving web of heat, but I could see a large, white cake, rectangular and three times the size of any regular birthday variety. Surrounding it were mounds of cupcakes and other sweets, as well as coins and beads.

Luis and Ana walked closer to the altar and turned left to greet *el padrino*, who was dressed in all white, which is a strict, year-long requirement of a priest who has just completed initiation. Timidly, I walked behind them, keeping my arms in. *El padrino* greeted me and I him. He asked us if we'd like a coffee. I didn't want to appear rude, but declined so that I wouldn't bounce from caffeine for the rest of the night.

His wife joined his side, greeting us warmly. She had a pretty face and an authentic smile and also wore all white in the form of a lace dress pulled off her shoulders with a head wrap of the same material. She pulled Luis close to her and nodded to me.

"*Bonita*," she said, directing her eyes to mine.

I blushed and looked to the ground as Luis touched my cheek with his finger. We lingered for a minute more but with so many people squeezing through, we moved toward the wall. My eyes were darts, shooting from side to side, wall to wall, floor to ceiling, trying to figure out what was going on around me. Luis laughed, noting how strange everything must have been.

Ana wanted to skirt the crowds and go outside. She turned back toward the door, and I followed suit, letting go of Luis's hand. Blocked in a crunch of people momentarily with Luis to my rear, I sensed something and looked back over my shoulder. Luis was on his knees on a straw mat, facedown, in the direction of the altar. Two candles, tall and white, were lit in front of him. He moved, propping himself with his right hand while his other went to his hip as it simultaneously rang a tiny bell. The house could have collapsed and I wouldn't have moved.

Luis changed the position of his hands, his left moving to the ground while his right took charge of the bell. He got up, walked to me, and smiled.

"Explain all of this to me," I all but begged in confused interest. He nodded and winked. "Outside."

Ana rinsed her hands in the rose water one more time before walking out. Trailing her, Luis and I looped the side of the house and stood on the small patch of grass while she perched on the salon's open windowsill, remaining an active member of the celebration without being swallowed by it. Luis pulled me into him and wrapped his hands around mine. This was an offering to his mom's saint, Ochún, who, he told me, is considered the happiest of all the orishas.

"You're Ochún," he told me.

"¿Cómo?" I asked in disbelief, as much so as my father when I told him that he and Luis are similar in many ways.

My hands frequently on my hips, cocked out a bit, I stand like her, he said.

169

OK.

More, she's kind and generous and loves to laugh. Ochún is hard to anger, but watch out if you do. She can be a bit of a sass. Much like my Libra predictions, she likes all things fine, is a lover of the arts, dance in particular, and is drawn to natural bodies of water.

Conveniently for Luis, Ochún is especially drawn to Changó. His lightning-and-fire saint is a feisty and powerful one. Red and white are the given colors, suddenly giving meaning to the similarly hued beaded bracelet that Luis sometimes wore.

Bells chimed again, in another act of worship before the altar. Two men suddenly stood in front of the offerings, one holding a violin and another a guitar. One of the more important rituals in Santería is a *bembé,* which invites the orisha to communicate with the community through drumming, singing, and dancing.

With notes rooted in bluegrass, the violinist began alone. In fluid precision, chords transitioned to classical, so moving I could have wept. The guitar slid in, raw and deeply honest. Its strings were invisible, singing a personal tale, far more intimate and profound than a new friend should be. Yet, I grabbed the leash and held tight.

As the two instruments melded, so too did all of the people in the room. They came together standing to face the altar and began to sway, forging a rolling and peaceful wave. The man with the guitar began to sing with a voice direct from the gods, in Yoruba. The volume rose and his voice was so clear my naked ear couldn't find a single glitch. I was so far inside the music that when it stopped it was like a bolt, the sudden silence. Though with barely a pause, the music segmented into sounds of pure, unadulterated joy.

This was why I had first come to Cuba.

The flowing wall of people began to break apart, each individual with rumba still evident in his or her steps. Cigars pushed into the air, like freestanding flags of freedom, and men and women puffed and passed them on, like joints at a college party. Someone busted out small, white plastic cups, each filled with smidgens of rum, which followed the cigars in close pursuit. Arms pushed hips and hips rolled to push out arms again and there wasn't a soul in sight who wasn't having a good time, Ana and I included. Luis, in his shyness, leaned against the wall and watched as we circled each other in our own mini rhythms of joy.

"*Baila, chica, baila!*" *El padrino* called to me through the window.

I grinned and held up my hands, my feet moving to the music.

Someone beckoned from inside: "Ana! Ana!" and she ran in, pausing to dip her hands in the plastic bowl once again.

Standing on the grass, looking in, I was out of place, but honored to be there. This was their world and they were allowing me an intimate peek.

Chapter 38

The Lost Boys of Cuba

The next day Luis and I were idle in the house, sleeping in. He only had to go to work that afternoon for a brief meeting. He drove away and I walked to the neighborhood grocery store. There weren't any fruits and veggies, as those are typically sold by vendors on the streets so the small rows were lined with mostly foreign products. Though the freezer bins advertised meat, they were empty. I grabbed Mexican cereal, similar to our Raisin Bran, and the yummy guayaba paste that I like so much, as well as chorizo, olives, and crackers that could be paired with cheese.

Ana's boyfriend, Abel, was going to celebrate his birthday with us that night so when I got back I made an antipasto plate and put it in the fridge, along with three red flowers I had picked off of a tree on the walk back. They would be for my hair after I showered.

Happy for cool water in such heat, I bathed and dressed in all black, threw on heels, and placed diamond studs in my ears. I pulled a taut ponytail at the base of my neck and plucked two of the flowers from their cool stems, fastening them to hide the black elastic. Luis liked my hair that way.

Abel came early so he, Ana, and I rocked in chairs in the parlor, toasting a beer to him. We talked until Luis arrived, my Spanish seemingly easier by the day. However, the heat was still a far reach for me. It could be rough at home, but this was unbearable. The windows were open, but nothing came in. I was slipping and sliding in my clothes and felt like I needed another bath, but there was no point to it.

At five Luis called to say he'd be there soon and at 7:20 he was downstairs. We were going to drop off the medical supplies I brought and would return for dinner around nine. I collected two mini tuna sandwiches I had made on crackers, as I knew he had probably skipped lunch, as he often did. Too busy, he frequently forgot to eat and would show up to the house shaking.

Luis was parked at the base of the steps. He was in a red polo shirt and dark glasses, his dark hair pushed back. I gave him a kiss and asked him if he was hungry. He said no, he had just eaten a pizza with tuna and that he brought some for me. I showed him the tuna sandwiches I had for him and we both laughed at our identical, but unsuccessful gestures.

After weaving through clusters of traffic and people, we reached Centro Havana. This area has the chaotic energy of a big city and is much more intense than Vedado, which in comparison feels like a suburb. On Avenida Italia, looking for Concordia, we slowed in front a church, not sure if it was the right one. A man came close to Luis's window and confirmed that we were in the right place. He showed us where to park.

"*Oye*," he said. "*Tienes Proscar?*"

Apologetic for not having the medicine he asked for, we parked and went inside. Luis asked how he knew we had medicine. I told him that the group met every Thursday night at seven and I was a foreigner. Easy math.

Going down a hallway a group of fifteen or so young men appeared in a room off to the left. The leader of the group waved for us to go in. Faces were bright and curious, but energy in the room was heavy. I assumed that most of the young men were HIV positive.

I told him that I had medical supplies and he said I should go upstairs and ask for Father Fernando. Above there was a room full of people busying themselves and almost in unison they nodded, "*Buenas, buenas.*"

Standing in front of a table full of covered dishes, an older gentleman with white hair and glasses came through a door to our right. I recognized him as Father Fernando from his photo on the website.

"*Buenas,*" I said.

"Hello," he responded in English with a thick Cuban accent.

"I have medical supplies."

"Yes, yes, come this way."

Around the table and people and cameras we went. I heard a couple of other men speaking English. They were Americans with white T-shirts, Rockport shorts, and backpacks. A journalist held a long-lensed camera.

The Father led us to the back. "This," he said, pointing to a four-paneled cabinet, "is our pharmacy."

A doctor in the room opened the doors to show a display of half-empty boxes with sprayed flaps. Inside were a loose mess of Advil, Tylenol, and other bottles. Luis asked if they had any Proscar for the man outside, as well as skin cream, for a family friend living with AIDS, noting how hard it was to find it, but they had neither.

The doctor broke my box open and began rummaging through, pulling out medicines to hold up into the light. Father Fernando handed me a receipt as proof of the donations, which was a condition of the visa I had purchased. On the bottom of the white square read: GOD BLESS YOU!

"This is the only English I know," he said with a large grin.

I thanked him.

We spoke briefly, as the journalist in me jumped out: How long had he been doing this work in Central Havana and why? Following the AIDS-related death of a friend's son in the States, Father Fernando was inspired to leave the US and bring help back to his country where there was still great prejudice.

He began the group with one small meeting seven years earlier. Free of politics or religion, he aimed to create support for young men who had become infected, mostly by working the streets as *jineteros*, or male prostitutes, with little or no family to turn to.

This support group, he said, was the only one of its kind, since very little information on AIDS was available at all in Cuba. Though rates were low, comparable to the rest of the world, cases grew every year by about five hundred on the island of eleven million.

The journalists in the main room came in to speak with the Father. We said our good-byes a second time and headed back down the stairs. In the car, I asked Luis if his friend living with AIDS ever attended a group like that one. He shook his head no.

Confirming the Father's views: "It's hard here," he said. "There is a lot of prejudice. If you have AIDS, people where you work, people on the street, are going to point. People assume they are going to die and so they stay away."

Chapter 39

Starstruck

The next morning, Luis was gone, but he had left freshly squeezed orange juice in the fridge for me, as he had done various other times.

He worked eighteen hours, but didn't complain of anything. When he got home that night, he beelined for the shower. Crisp and cleanly shaven, he sat next to me on the sofa.

"How was your day today, *Princesa*?" he asked sweetly. I found it ironic this was the name he latched on to for me. For one, I am anything but, and two, my mom also called me this.

I felt guilty even talking about it, seeing as I had done little, but I said, "Good." As with most days when he was away, I sat at the Nacional and wrote in my little, leather-bound book.

"What did you write today?"

I smiled without revealing anything.

"You have a lot to write about here in Cuba, no?"

"Volumes."

He smiled at me in a kooky sort of way.

"Yeeesss?" I asked.

He told me he never thought he'd find as much peace with anyone as he had with me. I felt the same way. He had a surprise for me.

Out of his pocket came a thick, amber wedding band, much richer in color than modern gold. I don't know anything about antique jewelry, but given the stateliness and elegance of the ring, I knew that it held a place in history. The story was that the ring had married five couples, all of whom stayed together. A good sales pitch or not, it was beautiful. Luis loved the ring and asked if he could cut my wedding band out of his.

A very large grin spread across my face. "I love that idea. Thank you."

We had the next few days to ourselves, as Luis had rearranged his schedule. Two were spent in magical Veradero, a beach town two hours from Havana. We hired a car to take us and rented a moped once there. Legally, Luis couldn't stay in a hotel, as those were for tourists only, and I created problems for Cubans who rent apartments, as they are not supposed to accept money from foreigners. We drove around for a couple of hours trying to find someone who could or would keep us both, but to no avail. Finally, I stayed out of sight while Luis paid for two nights at a petite, privately owned back apartment. If the landlady knew I was there, she never let on.

By day, we cruised along the small coastal highways, one of which led us to the end of a paved road. Luis parked on the edge of an undeveloped thicket. Sliding off he offered his hand, then led me through the underside of a wild mane of brush. Just on the other side was the most beautiful, virgin beach I had ever seen. To ourselves, we settled in the sand and later, splashed and played in the crystalline waters. It was spectacular.

Late in the afternoon, we headed for the apartment to shower and snooze, waking in the dark. Our evening was spent at Parque Josone, a sanctuary off the main strip, with a lake, rowboats, and a small walking bridge, which, strangely, intercepts an enclosure of ostriches, very Road Runner-like in their gestures.

Luis egged on a grumpy matriarch parrot, who sat on the corner of a bar on our way to dinner, into complete disarray. She cussed Luis up and down in Spanish for having bothered her at all. Passing the more formal restaurant on-site, we chose outdoor seating at the pizzeria next door, overlooking the water. We sat under the stars, hand-in-hand, at a private table off to the side. I felt light in a way that I hadn't been since my childhood.

A waiter came for drink orders and a rundown of specials, but I didn't take in a word: I was ensconced in the man's face. His image was as clear as it had been on TV so many times at home.

"That was Elián's dad?" I asked in total disbelief, after he'd walked off.

"*Sí*," Luis responded, unaffected.

To have the father of Elián González, splashed across our screens for the better part of 2000, wait on us, was unreal.

Still very clear in my mind were the desperate pleas for his son to be returned, the court battles, Gloria Estefan leading the charge to keep him in Miami, and then finally, the dramatic gun-pointed end with our troops forcing him from his relatives.

The dignified, mild-mannered Juan Miguel returned with our wine and water, followed shortly by a thin crust pizza. I never uttered a word, starstruck in a way I had not been by any celebrity sighting in Manhattan. I hadn't had too much of an opinion on the matter before, but seeing him, how gentle and kind he was, I knew the little boy belonged with his father.

Luis explained that since that time, Elián had become the figure of heroism in the Communist party, a favorite of Fidel's, by winning the small but ferocious war against the US.

"Give him a good tip," I whispered to Luis as he paid. He did, but I threw in another several bucks anyway before walking off.

Back in Havana, Luis took me to the National Theater to see native superstar Carlos Acosta, who is considered to be one of the world's greatest ballet dancers. On break from his role with the Royal Ballet in England, he soared on the stage under the direction of another great legend, Alicia Alonso, the premiere ballerina, who since 1948 has run the Ballet Nacional de Cuba. In what became my educational and cultural tour of Cuba, the following night we attended an art auction at the Canadian embassy with Luis's good friend, Alejandro Montesino, who is intricately connected to the government's cultural ranks. We walked the lawn behind the prim marble mansion and viewed creative originals and reprints of some of Cuba's most celebrated artists: Nelson Dominguez, Wifredo Lam, Roberto Fabelo, and Flora Fong while a Western-style auctioneer shot off prices.

The next day we visited Nelson Dominguez's gallery, the only self-owned in Cuba at that time. In Plaza San Francisco, one of five squares in Old Havana, his self-portraits ran the length of expansive walls; their power grabbed hold of me and tossed me violently around the room. Picasso came to mind; *this man is a genius*, I thought, and longed to fill my home and American museums with them. He wasn't ordinary and as Luis explained, he is, to my credit, referred to as the Picasso of their country.

The meal with Nelson was interesting, if not strange, with his much younger, silent wife by his side. Midway through, a young fan approached Nelson for an autograph. A good hit to his healthy ego, he pulled an unused napkin from his lap, dabbed a fork into his half-consumed cup of coffee, and streamed a drawing with a few more dips. He signed it and sent the kid on his way. Before we left, he handed me a small drawing with a personal inscription.

Later that night, we entered the front gate of Luis's former stepfather's home where we were to visit for the night and *poof*, I was doused in a wash of white powder in the dark. Startled, I laughed.

"What in the world was that?" I asked Luis.

With a rather large, empathetic smile, he explained: *cascarilla*, a white powder prepared by *santeros,* is made from eggshells.

"He thinks it protects you from bad spirits."

"I guess we can all use that," I said, wiping the musty mess from my face. I laughed again on my way inside, wondering what in the world I had gotten myself into.

Chapter 40

Lockout

I returned to Savannah, only to plan my next trip within weeks. I was still living at home with no rent to pay, yet all the cash I made headed straight to savings for my next trip and telephone bills, which were mounting quickly. At almost one dollar a minute and one to two conversations nightly, the bills were creeping into the hundreds each month, but I couldn't help myself. I couldn't put the phone down.

Between the calls and regular bills, it would be a couple of months before I could get back to Cuba. By November I was delirious to see Luis and again flew directly from Miami, on the wing of my individual license, but not before putting in an official request for paperwork from DC. Luis and I had a lot of information to piece together on this trip.

As we sat at his dinner table, I painstakingly filtered through each line with him, filling in appropriate items regarding his family. On paper, our convergence appeared to be an accident. Names like Abelardo, Macho, Felicia, and Ana Luisa dot his Cuban lineage while Ralph, Margaret, Henry, Fannie, Martha, Lorraine, and James paint mine.

This was the first time that he had made real mention of his father's side. His dad's sister he knows, but nothing about grandparents or beyond. On my dad's side, my grandmother spent tireless hours—forty years plus—tracing our history to the 1300s, with a master book that now sits in the Georgia Historical Society library and includes original documents on our Germanic and British ancestors she tracked in courthouses throughout Georgia, South Carolina, and Europe.

I never questioned the connection between Luis and me, but there were times that these sorts of differences were striking. Never in my childhood had I created this scenario.

Just before I left, he gave me an official copy of his birth certificate and two passport photos. Each time I left was harder than the time before, not understanding why we had to be separated. I sat on the plane with uncontrollable streams running down my cheeks. I wiped them away, only to have identical trails follow in their footsteps.

Once back, I sent paperwork off and waited. And waited. I had accepted a full-time day position, which would give me more stability and a consistent salary, but also created structure to which I needed to adhere. Without being able to take off on a moment's notice or go to Cuba for weeks at a time, every day was a challenge to stay put, to focus, and to be responsible. Luis and I had to have long-term vision, as we both knew it was the only way we could be together.

A routine began on my part, rather strict in its form. Monday through Friday, I got up, ate breakfast, and packed exactly four small meals to carry me through my workday, from nine to six, as well as a gym bag. At the six o'clock mark, I headed straight for the gym, worked out, and then headed home to make my small, healthy dinner. I then sat and watched TV, savoring my one limitless treat that I allowed myself—strawberries with mounds of Cool Whip.

Every night I called Luis and ached. It took everything in me to get off the phone, even after an hour. Always uncomfortably aware that someone could be listening to our phone calls on his side of the world, our conversations swayed mostly to our personal, daily lives. It was rare that we touched on politics or censorship in Cuba.

On occasion, I crossed a line, angrily reacting to something I heard or read in the news, about how Castro and Bush were ready to take one another's heads off, or some wacko new law on the island. Sometimes Luis would comment, but mostly he went silent, and I knew I had said something I shouldn't have. After a long pause, he suggested that we talk in person.

It was so difficult for me to bear the weeks ahead of us, a contributing factor, certainly, to my almost vigilant daily regimen. I was desperate to break free and sprint to Cuba, so I leaned hard on my newfound schedule, a way of reigning myself in so I wouldn't be tempted to follow my instincts and run, run, run to Luis.

For all of my life, my mother had been credited for my personality, which is largely an artistic one, but not enough credit, perhaps, had been given to my dad, who is the most disciplined human being I have ever come across. He is all heart and loves to laugh, but he will always do what he is supposed to do, including the most tedious of chores, before playing. I am not as capable as he, but when I needed to access that part of me that resounds fully in him, I can grab it. And I did. I stuck to work and exercise, with an occasional outing on the weekends with friends, and by December, in my much slimmer silhouette, I began shopping for a wedding dress.

At night, Luis got daily updates on the status of our visa, which was the same every day—*nada*. Absolutely no information. Every morning and every afternoon at work I called the US Visa Center hotline to check the status of our case, typing in the unique set of capital letters and numbers given to us by Homeland Security, which I had committed to memory. It was a quick call and response. I came to hate the voice of the recording on the other end. Had she a soul, she would have been my real-life nemesis. I would receive something in the mail within four to six weeks, she told me.

At times, I waited hours to speak with a live person, who offered no more assistance or regard for human feelings than the she-bot. Four to six weeks, she reiterated. This would become months.

To further complicate matters, President Bush pushed even tighter restrictions with Cuba. In a near lockout, the visas I had coasted on previously were unavailable; the verbal wars between the two countries were far more aggressive.

Still, at the end of December, I escaped via Cancun on a quick three-day trip to Cuba. Like representatives of our countries, Luis and I were increasingly agitated. Our future was on hold indefinitely until we got that hot little visa in our hands, a fact that any number of people at home were all the more ready to point out.

Repeatedly I was asked by friends and strangers alike, bouncing my predicament around like cocktail party conversation: "What will you do if he can't get here? If he can't get his visa?"

I offered only one response. "He will."

"But what if it doesn't work?"

"It will."

"But?"

"It will."

"But?"

"It will. It's going to work."

I believed it. The idea that the visa wouldn't go through never entered my brain, not even once. I only had to forge ahead and stay on top of the system that would allow him to come.

One night out, however, I bumped into an old school friend who worked for our local congressman. She suggested I contact a woman in her office named Trish, who might be able to dig and find out what was taking so long. First thing Monday morning I called.

Trish had worked with the congressman for years, but there was no sense that she had been in politics that long. She had a great sense of humor and immediately put me at ease. Instinctively, I trusted her when she said that she would do anything she could to help me. I was asked to put in writing what I lacked and fax it to her.

"Thank you," I said. "Thank you so much."

To this stranger, who assisted people like me, day in and day out, I wasn't an anomaly. Nothing peculiar about it, I was just a young person in love with someone who happened to be from Cuba. I shared with her as much.

"It's OK, honey," she said. "You call me anytime, even if you just need to talk. Or if you need a hug, just come in the office!"

I didn't get by the office for a long time, but I did call her from time to time, for as much emotional support as legal advice. Shortly after my first call to her, I received a notice of approval, which allowed us to move to the next step. It was a baby step, but it was important, logistically and psychologically. This was something tangible that Luis and I could hold on to. We were integrated in the system and, in theory anyway, moving forward.

We were on to the next set of paperwork. I filled out information and collected more of whatever they needed. Shoe and sock size, check. What Luis liked to eat for breakfast, check. Was he a member of Communist Party? No, check. Whatever they wanted, I did it and sent it in with the next check payable to the United States.

Once again, to the land of waiting. Daily, I continued to call the visa hotline and daily, I was rebuffed. There was one particular day, standing outside my office, that I almost smashed my little, black cell phone into the Savannah Grey bricks in front of me. I just wanted to scream bloody hell, why was this so f**!$!**!! difficult! Godddddddddddddddddddddd!

Trish was going to see what she could do. Though I trusted her efforts more than mine, I didn't expect miracles. Still, I held out hope.

I was agitated as it was, because my brother and I were about to head to New York to bury our mom.

Chapter 41

To Mom, Love *Princesa*

Early January 2003

I saw you today at the gym. I wanted it to be you. She had
your hair and your cute celestial nose, your nonathletic
stance on the treadmill, your pale reflection, your softness. I
tried to leave, but you pulled me in. I needed it to be you for
just a few moments. The blond fifty-something was unaware
of my focus, but finally, I pulled myself away before she was.

Tonight I came home and found two checks—one for
Walter and one for me. It was money from one of your
accounts that Jim should have kept, but didn't. Recently, all
I have been able to think about are phone bills full of calls to
Cuba, flights both to Cuba and to New York for your service,
and car payments. But you stepped in and took care of that
this month. Thank you.

I miss you so much and I still think of you every day. I
want to talk to you every day. I wish you could see my wedding gown. I think you would love it. I think you would love
Luis. We all miss you terribly, but we're hanging in there. We
still need closure so we'll have a service on your birthday. I

can't believe it's been two years. Jim said you don't want a headstone, which I don't entirely understand, but respect.

Walter's doing great and I'm so proud of him. Jim's going to his fiftieth college reunion and I'm getting married to the most wonderful man. But I guess maybe you know all of this. Or do you? Where are you, anyway?

I love you, Mom. Wish you were here.

Love, *Princesa*

Chapter 42

Graveside

A week later

We flew in from separate parts of the country—I came from Savannah and my brother from the University of Montana—and I stayed with my old roommate, Jacque, while Walter headed to our aunt's, an hour north of the city. On the morning of the ninth, the day before my mom's birthday, Jacque rode the train to New Jersey with me. I hadn't been back to my mom's house since she had died.

Jim picked us up at Convent Station and I was happy to see him, as was Jacque. When we pulled up to the house, the coffeepot in my stomach tipped over, sloshing madness all over my system. As I walked through the door, I knew I was crossing into dark, dangerous territory. It was a wild jungle where I was outnumbered by memories. I did not want to be there.

The front of the house, which includes the foyer, the kitchen, and the dining room, was manageable, as I had no specific thoughts attached to them. Only: "Mom, do you think you should be drinking coffee?"

"What's it going to do—kill me?" and she laughed that naughty little laugh, a bright twinkle still in her eye, and sipped her morning cup.

Shaking my head: "You're sick. Absolutely sick in the head," and I laughed with her.

But as I moved in and passed the bathroom door to the right, the harbor of the living room to the left, and finally the small family room where she had died in her homebound hospice bed, I didn't know how I was going to make it in that house until the next morning. Jim took us out to dinner and roused us as always, so at minimum, the night was filled with good times.

Careful not to drink more than one glass of wine at dinner—I couldn't handle feeling any more out of control than I already did—we headed straight to bed once back in the house. On my way up, I noticed a sturdy, white box on the dining room table that wasn't there earlier in the day. I knew it was my mom. I felt queasy, but never stopped to take an extra glance. Upstairs, I took the twin bed where I always slept and Jacque took my mom's. Inundated with flashes, I turned on the TV to help drown them.

"Are you OK?" Jacque asked.

"Not really. Just want to get through tomorrow and go home," though I didn't even know what that meant.

New York felt like home in so many ways, but I didn't know how to be there. Mom was home, but she wasn't there. I wanted to be with Luis, but couldn't. I was so confused. Why was it so hard to just be? Jacque fell asleep, but I was restless and ended up watching TV for another two or three hours.

In the dark, I walked the stairs down toward the dining room. With only minimal light from the foyer, I moved toward the box, full of my mom's ashes. I must have stared at it for a solid minute before I picked it up. It was much heavier than I thought it would be. I put it back down, feeling unsteady. Another minute passed and I tried to slide the top off, but it wouldn't budge. Suddenly, I was nauseous, really nauseous, and ran back up the stairs to the bathroom, where I threw up. I stayed on the second floor the rest of the night.

The next morning, Mom's birthday, Jim had the box in an over-size Valentine's Day bag, which sat by the front door. I didn't want pageantry, but this seemed a little too practical to me. I ignored it with vigilance, as if it were a live person sitting, gun in hand, ready to take me out.

That morning, I got an email from Allison, who, by then, was on the other side of the world, in South Korea teaching English:

Subject: much to my regret
Date: Fri, 10 Jan 2003 15:47:28 -0500

I know you were kind of emotional about leaving and going up to New York. I am sorry that you are nervous and freaked about your mom's funeral but this is a necessary step in order to continue with the mending process.

God, that sounds so clinical and dry. What I mean is that ceremonies suck but we need them in order to get on with things and say good-bye and . . . kind of like hello. Like you are checking on her to see what's up. Like cemeteries. They are there so we can hang out with our loved ones and feel comfortable visiting their earthly remains . . . even though you carry your mom's spirit inside of you all of the time.

I love you so much and miss you. You are my best and strongest friend.

By the way, I have been having weird dreams about you and Luis. I won't go into detail but it entails you in lingerie and heels cooking eggs in the kitchen while he dances naked around the house.

Weird, huh? Poor Luis. He is going to go bananas when he meets your insane friends.

You are a strong, groovy chick. Try not to go nutty and start throwing things . . . but if you have to, do it. I hope Jim is handling things OK. It seems like he gets a little kooky when it comes to you and your mom. I think you may remind him so much of your mom that he wants to hold on just a bit longer. Try to understand but be firm about what you know your mother would want . . . which is to be laid to rest . . . right?

I love you. Survive New York only to love Cuba.

Write me when you get back to the States.

Love, Allie

On the drive to the cemetery, the box sat under my seat. Jim, Jacque, and I rambled about theater, symphonies, and Jim's arthritis, but our conversations could only distract me so much from the bag, full of my mom, just below.

When we arrived, Jacque, Zia, and my family waited by the front gate while Jim and I went inside the office to finalize paperwork and to pay, which seemed weird and cold to me. I had the box with me and clutched it under my arm, walking numbly down the hall behind the priest, who had joined us. I was starting to lose it, but sucked it up as much as I could. There was nothing to say, but I couldn't have talked even if I wanted to. Sadness is so heavy.

We drove behind the priest to the site with the others in tow. The gloomy sky had cleared and the full sun was out. It was strikingly beautiful in its clear blue and yellow, but bitterly cold. Mom's spot was on top of a hill, and rolling green space was all around. As far as cemeteries go, it's very pretty, but I couldn't find the beauty.

Our small group chatted among themselves in hushed, respectful tones. I started to cry and walked away from everyone, careful not to slip on the icy grass. In front of me was a small square, deep and empty, where a plot of grass had been. I felt just as empty.

Walter appeared at my side and looped his arm in mine. The priest gently asked if I wanted to put the box in the ground before or after he spoke. I looked at Walter, feeling lost, and did a limp shrug with my shoulders.

"Now, I guess."

He took the box from me and handed it to a woman who placed my mom into the space; it was more than I could take. Walter remained steady through it all.

The priest said a lot of words that didn't mean anything to me. He didn't know my mom, so it sounded false and contrived. I was offended, but didn't want to be angry, so I drowned him out. I said good-bye, or hello, as Allison aptly put it, in my own, silent way.

My eyes closed and I let her know that I thought about her every day, that I missed her terribly, and that I loved her so much. Every day was still a challenge to accept that she was gone. The ceremony was short and then we, one by one, put down roses, pink and red, that Aunt Cathi brought with her. I told Mom happy birthday and good-bye and turned around. Jim was standing there. He came straight to me and hugged me tightly.

When I got home, I realized that a chapter had closed officially while another was wide open.

Chapter 43

Friends and the Curious Case of the Speed Bump

There was a wedding to plan.

Luis and I decided on April 26 in Havana. I wrote out a Save-The-Date, unlike most, with the 1, 2, 3s on how to get to Cuba legally. I was available anytime to help. Over a hundred invites were sent in the US, knowing only a handful of close friends and minimal family would go.

Luis, on his end, was churning the wheels, trying to make things happen. No easy task in Cuba, where getting anyone to finalize anything was nothing short of a miracle.

I visited him in February, but this was to be the last visit before we married. With me were two of my best friends, Jacque and Susan. They were there to see Cuba, sure, but I knew more than anything they were there to meet Luis.

We did the standard touristy bits, visiting Old Havana and Colón Cemetery, walking the Malecón and drinking mojitos and cappuccinos at Hotel Nacional. The girls couldn't speak Spanish and Luis of course spoke no English, but they slowly connected through howls of laughter as Susan belted show tunes in the backseat and we made stops for pizza near the beach. Luis and I took long distance photos of them, hands thrown in the air, glowing in the chilly, afternoon breeze.

To round out their experience, a couple of days later, coasting over a speed bump in Havana, a police siren brought us all to a stop in a residential neighborhood. The officer asked Luis to step out of the car and go across the street where two more policemen stood. Lunch shot to my throat. What was happening? Not a sound moved between the three of us in the car, virtual stones in terror.

The officer, fitted with a large gun on his hip, came around to my open window and started drilling questions: How much was I paying the young man to drive? I panicked, played dumb, and pretended not to speak Spanish. But I think he sensed I did, driving further questions to me alone: How much gas had I put in his car? Where were we going? Were we staying at the young man's house and at what cost? I played the same routine, but he wasn't buying it and my hands were dripping.

Finally, Luis shot across the street and told me it was okay to tell the officer the truth. Hesitantly, I explained in Spanish that Luis and I were engaged, showing the ring on my finger to prove it. My friends and I were all guests at his home. After a brief exchange between Luis and the officer, he hopped back in the car and we drove off. Still, no one spoke on the return trip to the apartment.

Following that trip Susan wrote a letter to my dad, confiding that she had shared his concerns about my relationship, but all she needed to see was the way Luis looked at me and she wasn't worried anymore.

Chapter 44

A Havana Wedding
and the Canadian Chickens

By April, our guest list had dwindled considerably, with only twenty Americans heading to Cuba. Some were flying to Miami, then directly to Havana, while others flew in from New York and via Mexico. We made arrangements for some to stay at the Hotel Nacional while others were to rent rooms at a property just across the street.

As a kid, I was never a Barbie Doll dreamer. I didn't lose hours on tiaras or wedding day visions. But in the weeks before we married, I did find myself doing uncharacteristically girlie things. I felt strange and princess-like modeling wedding dresses. The dress was easy to find and only the third I tried on. The headpieces were even stranger and Becky had to help me decide on that. And seeing as there would be no one to help with our makeup and hair in Cuba, she and I went for lessons with a professional.

On the night that I began to pack, I became nervous for the first time. It was four days before I was to marry and I began to worry about wedding details and the overall flow of getting guests to the island safely and on time.

Then there was my dress to contend with. I was completely paranoid that my getup for the big day might be viewed as a gift or random item for the taking in Cuban customs. I packed nonessential items in a suitcase to be checked, but painfully, I stepped aside as Becky prudently rolled my wedding dress into a narrow sliver, an oversize Cuban cigar, the underworks and all. I don't know how she did it, but it was unbearable to watch.

She assured me that her steamer would take out the very large creases that were certainly going to be set before the big day. I took a deep breath and said, "OK." *This is insane*, I thought. I had also done the same with a suit I had bought for Luis in New York. Those, packed with our shoes and my makeup, traveled with me in a miniature suitcase that I rolled onto the plane and stored safely above me.

Walter and Becky traveled with me, using the visas I had helped arrange. My dad couldn't commit to Cuba. His discomfort with the powers of the communist country won. I was sad, but not angry. I knew that for him not to go to my wedding, sentiments were high. Besides, in typical practicality, he had been the one to encourage us to elope and use his monetary gift for a down payment on a house.

We all passed through customs in a breeze, with no detection of the dress or suit, which were topped by sheets, and walked out into the madness that is the Cuban airport. My eyes darted around quickly to locate Luis, who stood just outside the gate. Not having seen him in over three months, I had to process him in the flesh. We spoke daily for hours, but to see and hug him was emotionally huge, exacerbated, of course, by the fact that we would marry in a matter of days.

Luis was tiny. He told me he had been working out daily like me, but I had no idea he had dropped thirty pounds. The suit I bought was going to swallow him whole.

I stepped aside. "Walter, this is Luis. Luis, Walter," I said.

Luis stuck out his hand to Tall Walter's.

"*Hola,*" said Walter, returning the shake. "*Cómo estás?*"

Luis smiled and nodded. "*Bien, gracias.*"

He hugged Becky and she gave him a kiss on the cheek. Thank God for my nice family. That so could have gone another way.

After the intros we hopped in the red Bug, dropped off their bags at the Hotel Nacional, and went to Luis's house so they could meet Ana, who had cooked a big, gorgeous meal for us all. No one could understand one another, and I translated as best I could, but even when my abilities failed, it didn't stop us all from laughing throughout dinner. Our families were finally together, and Luis and I were no longer confined to my head.

Luis and Melanie, Hotel Nacional, April 25, 2003 (*Corinna Robbins*).

After dinner we took Becky and Walter to the hotel and had a drink out back. I could tell they had touched that same something that I had my first trip to Havana. It was pure magic in the air. Though, with too much to do in the next days, we didn't make it a late night. Guests would begin to arrive the next day and Luis had set up a tour for those who wanted it so we could hustle and take care of things.

Walter joined the guests while Becky came with us as we spent a good amount of time in the car, racing from one venue to another to check on various items. Planning a wedding in Cuba is like nothing most can imagine.

A typical Cuban wedding is an informal affair, followed by food, rum, and good music, of course. The government picks up the tab for the reception so a number of people get married just to have a party, annulling it soon thereafter. But Luis had a different vision. He wanted our wedding his way, and perhaps, Luis is the only person I know who could have pulled off what he did.

An acquaintance of his, they called him Guajiro, or Mountain Man, worked at the Hotel Nacional back then. One afternoon, Luis ordered a mojito and a cigar from him, sitting at the outdoor bar.

"I want to have our wedding reception here," he said.

Guajiro all but jumped. "You want it here?" he spurted. "You want to have your wedding reception here? I'm going to help you have it here," hitting his open hand on the bar's wooden top.

A week later, Guajiro called. "I have the salon, but it's small. Not gonna do. I want you to be where Compay Segundo plays!"

He was referring to the much larger ballroom, just off the back gardens.

"And behind the columns, we're going to put an open bar, not a box!" alluding to the customary bottles of rum that are passed around parties.

For that bar, he was going to arrange getting beer and wine, a slightly complicated matter since, as I previously mentioned, rum is the running choice on the island. Then he got into the chicken.

"And I want the chickens from Canada—the big ones."

Guajiro wasn't having any of the Brazilian chickens, the small ones that Cuba likes to ship in. And, "Here, everyone here eats one thing. Well, my friend, your guests are going to eat two! This isn't a factory job get-together," he preached to a solo choir. "No, *mi amigo*, you are going to have chicken *and* fish!"

When Luis asked about getting bronze candelabras for the tables, Guajiro had a maid from the hotel search for only the candelabras on site that stood straight (and quite a task that was, I must say) and asked her to make them shine. Since Luis, as a Cuban, wasn't allowed to stay in the hotel at that time, somehow, some way, Guajiro arranged this, too.

"But promise me, for *Changó, por tu Mamá*, that you won't tell the manager of the hotel that you are a *taxista*! If he asks you what you do, change the conversation. Tell him you work at the University of Havana."

Several years later, when Ana saw the manager, he asked if Luis is still a scientist.

Guajiro had become key to our wedding. A true angel. Luis stayed in touch with him on a regular basis to facilitate all that he could while also juggling a gazillion other details—the buses to take guests to the wedding, the dinner rehearsal at a lovely, out-door restaurant, the wine that would be served there, and getting permission that no one ever tries to obtain in Havana.

He put in a request for us to get married at Castillo del Morro, the sixteenth-century military fortress in Old Havana that I spied on that first ride along the Malecón with Cynthia and Luis. The problem was that as one of the more important historical mon-uments in Cuba and a military base, El Morro was off limits to an *Americana.* Luis was told that no one had ever been married there before and he would have to seek special permission. Though on the verge of impossible, Luis remained determined, dogmatic even, about having it there.

He wanted our wedding to include the fort's history, beauty, and formal pomp with our own horse carriage and parade of soldiers, the same ones who, to this day, dress in Spanish colonial wear and sound off cannons at precisely nine o'clock each evening, carrying forward the centuries-old tradition of warning Havana's citizens to stay indoors and away from night pirates.

When the local magistrate mentioned that there are typically only two soldiers available for wedding ceremonies, Luis, in a hush, said, "I want eight."

"*Ay, mi hijo!* You and your American!" she gushed. "You with your American and me with *mis pelucas.*"

The wigs. The wigs! Only two colonial white wigs were in good enough shape to put on the heads of the soldiers. Luis spins magic when he's on and he worked it. He offered to help pay to clean them. Anything, he'd do just about anything to get married there. Finally, he bartered with our tale. Cubans live for stories and the woman fell deeply into ours. Onboard, she called the department in Cuba's version of the White House that oversees religious ceremonies to request specific permission for a Cuban and an American to get married on base. Three days before the wedding, we still didn't have an answer. I was sick-to-my-stomach nervous. Becky asked me what we were going to do if we couldn't get married there. I had no idea and trusted that Luis had something else lined up. I couldn't think about it.

In the meantime, Becky and I went to see the Cake Lady. We sat in the salon of the ranch-style home and flipped through pages of cake photos, as well as flower arrangements. After making decisions, she assured us that both the flowers and the cake would be at the wedding, wherever that might be, and the reception hall. There was no management control, no one to hold accountable. I had to trust her. I felt sick again.

We did get word, shortly thereafter, that we had been approved for the military base. So while we were with the Cake Lady, Luis bolted to take care of the invitations, which he would hand deliver to eighty friends and family members the day before the wedding, seeing as there is no postal service in Cuba.

A computer whiz Luis called El Flaco for his slim build agreed to the task of invitation design.

"I want something old-fashioned," Luis told El Flaco. "I don't want any of the cookie-cutter square invites."

Luis wanted to create invitations that resembled something like a scroll, on the same sort of paper used when mail was delivered horseback-style.

"It's a great idea," El Flaco said. "But what kind of paper are we going to use?"

Wax. Luis wanted wax.

"*Ven acá*," he said, looking Luis directly in the eye. "Do you know how hard it is to find wax paper on the island?"

"*Sí*," said Luis, with that killer Aries charm fully on. The poor soul was hooked and reeled.

Not only was he was ready to do it, but he was going to do it. At 1:00 a.m., Luis got a phone call. The man found the paper.

"*Encontré papel! ENCONTRÉ PAPEL! VEN.*"

He had found the paper through someone who knew someone in the Havana Archives department and insisted that Luis go right then to look at it.

"*Haceré*, don't get divorced this year," they guy joked when Luis walked in the door.

The paper was perfect, but the guy called again the next day, out of breath, saying that the ink wasn't catching on the paper. Luis ran to his assistance and together they worked it out.

The rest of the time was nuts. The day of the wedding, the Cake Lady asked Luis to get some ingredient for the meringue, or the cake would fall apart in the heat. That morning, as I sat with friends and family in the back garden of the Nacional, Luis hurried back and forth, clearly ragged, with a near beard on his face. I felt badly for him and asked what I could do, but he told me it was just easier for him to do all.

Later, upstairs in Becky's room, my girlfriends and I all got ready. Beck and Allie stayed out of sight as they used the small steamer to get the deep creases out of my dress. It had been hanging for three days, but the work to be done on it was sizable. For the first time, I began to act the part of a slightly neurotic bride. I laughed at their jokes, which they were doling out to keep the energy light, but from time to time I took the bait.

Allie had taken on the unenviable task of assembling my loads of short hair layers into a tousled bun, which would hide well under my veil. She sprayed a hefty amount of product on the back end of my hair, but when she tried to do the same up front, I snapped.

"Not so much!"

Her eyes rolled and she tried to calm me down. I apologized for being an ass, making fun of my absurd behavior. Sweet Al, she did a great job on my hair, just like a pro. I must say I did a good job on my makeup. Beck and the girls all helped me get on my dress, which was spectacular. I don't know how they did such a good job. I told everyone to go get ready themselves and that Beck and I would see them at the service.

About twenty minutes before Luis and I were to marry, Walter called to say that the buses to pick up all the guests had not arrived.

Wedding day car, April 26, 2003 (*Corinna Robbins*).

Short with him (I still feel guilty), I asked the only one of our friends who spoke Spanish to get every guest into a cab and tell the driver exactly where to go.

Upon confirmation that all of the Americans were in transport, I made my way to the entrance of the hotel and looked down onto a cream-colored 1925 Ford with a black soft top, resting on the driveway's Hotel Nacional emblem. It was deeply cared for, not a note of discoloration on its frame. A delicate, white bow perched on the front headlight and drew long tiers of ribbon to smaller white blossoms on two side mirrors. Luis had gone through so much trouble to make everything perfect and this was the most beautiful thing I had ever seen.

I was getting married!

The driver greeted me and offered his hand to help me down the marble steps and then up into the backseat of the car. Walter and Becky joined me. As we drove along the Malecón, the ocean brought perspective. How far I had come.

(*Terry McNeal*)

We wove in and around the cobblestones until we stopped at a circle. From there we were moved from the car to a horse and buggy with a female driver, fitted in a black hat and red tailcoat. In a slow clip clop, we wound through the colonial fort until we reached the small chapel. Walter and Becky got out before me to take their seats in the church.

Moments later, I floated as I walked to the doorway. A violinist played "Ave Maria" in the back corner of the church, signaling my entrance, per our rehearsal the day before. I focused on Luis, standing at the front of the aisle, looking at me with such wonder. His eyes are what I remember most. They were huge, boring into me.

The sensation of seeing him while passing my American family and friends, who sat next to Luis's, was entirely strange and exhilarating.

Luis took my hand as I stood next to him. Quietly, he said, "You're beautiful."

"Thank you," I returned, gently.

Two priests stood in front of us. The female priest spoke in Spanish and to my surprise, her male counterpart translated all into English. It was a brief ceremony that ended as Luis and I were joined with a band of white cloth. We kissed and that was that. We were married! The priests led us to a table covered in white lace and tropical flower arrangements. The Cake Lady had pulled through.

After signing our names to a register, we were official in the eyes of the church: Mr. and Mrs. Luis Simón. It was a requirement that Luis and I marry in the United States within three months of his arrival, which we would do at the local courthouse, but as far as we were concerned, that was an afterthought.

Colonial Redcoats stood just outside the chapel, their muskets crossed in an upside down V. Luis and I were lifted into the carriage and rode slowly through the fortress, stopping a handful of

Wedding day, El Morro Cabaña, April 26, 2003 (*Corinna Robbins*).

times for photographer's shots. I could sense that Luis was uptight. There was still, in his mind, much that could go wrong, though the wigs were in shape, clean and fitted on the eight soldiers who saluted us as we made the final lap of our ride. One off his list, anyway.

When we reached the guest congregation area near the fort's entrance, we quickly realized that several of the private cars Luis had hired to carry them all were no-shows. The sky was growing dark and our driver all but begged us to get in the backseat of the Ford, as he unlatched the top hatch to push it back and down. Luisito, by then, squeezed his little body in between us, fascinated with the antique latch settings.

We helplessly watched as our family and friends crammed into the few cars there. Happily, they waved and told us not to worry.

Wedding day, Hotel Nacional (*Corinna Robbins*).

I saw Luis's jaw tighten, in what he may have presumed was a premonition of what was to come. I'm sure he imagined the cake melting, flyaway Canadian chickens, a nonfunctioning open bar, or a salsa band that would never show. He didn't tell me until after the fact, but he wasn't even sure that they were going to let us in the chapel that day, permission or not.

I held his hand over Luisito's lap in my best efforts to will him to relax. Gray clouds quickly turned into black as we rode along the Malecón. I hoped we'd make it to the reception dry, but really, I didn't care. People cheered and clapped from the street and we waved and smiled back. The rain held and we quickly took pictures in the back of the Hotel Nacional.

In the reception area, a large room where Compay Segundo had played so many times, two bars were set up, gorgeous flowers were in place, and the wedding cake was on a stand. The musicians were onstage, testing their mikes, and as we learned later, chicken and fish with their accompanying rice, beans, and other dishes were all served well by attentive waiters.

After dinner, we headed for the dance floor. Barefoot with my skirt bunched in my hands, I celebrated as the sky fell in and water came in hard streams from various points of the roof. Men with mops raced across the floor in their best drying efforts, but none of us cared, Luis included by then, as we danced for the better part of the night.

Late into the night, Luis and I took the elevator up to the eleventh floor. Rose petals in front of the door led through the foyer and into the shape of a heart on our bed.

Shoes off, Luis wriggled his cuff links loose while I looked outside the window and down onto the moonlit gardens.

Luis walked behind me and looped his arms around, folding his hands at my waist. He kissed the back of my neck.

"*Te amo*," Luis whispered in my ear.

My left hand raised and stroked the side of his head, which was resting on my shoulder. A slight turn of my neck and we were lip to lip.

"*Te amo también*," I returned, water in my eyes. "I love you too."

Chapter 45

Tobacco, Mangoes, and the Horseback *Cafecito*

Many of my American guests headed back home the next day while a few traveled on in Cuba. Luis and I spent the next three days in the countryside of Pinar del Río, on the western end of the island, in a small house situated on a *finca*, one of Cuba's farms.

To go from the madness of the previous days to that felt like we were the only people on the planet. In our room of open-shuttered windows, we woke to chirping birds and roosters crowing. We rocked in chairs and swayed in hammocks on the front porch, which sat among an exquisite overflow of vines and bright red and violet tropical flowers with their clean and sweet scent.

Mountains created a long-distance panorama and a walk on a dirt path and small bridge over a pond brought the sound of a small rush of water. In front of the fall, we ate fried chicken and handmade, matchstick French fries under a mob of stars, a cool breeze off-setting the night. We were so happy it was ridiculous.

The second day in, Luis managed to get me on a horse, something I hadn't done since I was a young child. My horse was mild-mannered, really a bit too slow, but that suited me just fine.

We trailed slowly off the *finca* and down the paved road until our guide detoured through grassy fields and plots of corn, tobacco, and mango, littered with dilapidated, wooden homes. Chickens, pigs, and cows strutted and grazed their rows, but humans were scant.

Coming to a halt at the face of a straw hut, Luis put his hand out to help me off the horse and I slid with a thud to the ground. He disappeared inside, calling me to come in. Pitch-black inside, I turned on the bright light of our video camera. I nearly jumped at the sight of what looked like scores of bats hanging upside down. As my vision focused, I saw the outline of tobacco leaves, which, as Luis explained, were drying until ready to be processed.

We walked back outside and it began to drizzle. As we hopped back on the horses (I was starting to look like a real pro), we trotted back down the same trail until we hit a minor incursion with overgrown roots. My horse was not going to budge. Luis and the guide were instructing me what to do, but I wasn't so polished in equestrian Spanish. Amused, Luis hopped off his horse to come pull mine down. But that old horse still was not going to move. I had to get off and let Luis ride him out, which he did with immense ease.

I asked the guide if he lived in the area and learned that indeed, we were going to pass his house at any moment. We veered off the main path and cut through a series of homes until we landed, quite literally, on his doorstep. His wife came out and handed us *un cafecito,* and we threw back the three sips sitting on top of our horses. Off we went.

Rain began to come down hard and my white clothes turned a nice shade of burnt orange with patches of dark gray. Starting to chill, with my ponytail matted to my head in various segments, I was reminded of being ten years old and sliding down clay mountains in North Carolina with my dad and brother. That was a happy, carefree time in my life and so was this.

On the fourth morning, we returned to Havana to see Luisito off to Guatemala. My heart ached for Luis having to say goodbye to his son. After spending several good hours with him at the house and the airport, Luis was quiet on our drive to Veradero, where we would spend the next three days. It rained most of the time, save one gorgeous afternoon at the beach, but neither of us cared much. I am always touched by the beauty of Cuba's ocean and sands, regardless of the weather.

Chapter 46

Acceptance

Leaving Luis was torturous, and as much as I tried to integrate back into work, it was near shell shock. I functioned numbly in daily work efforts, feeling dismayed. Life seemed to be on permanent pause.

We survived the next nine months, emotionally and financially, with four kamikaze trips I made to the island, funded completely by the work of Cuban artists.

After meeting with our artist friend, Alejandro Montesino, I carried his bold and colorful canvases, rolled under my arm from Havana, through Mexico, and back to Savannah, in what was a test sales run. I unfurled the paintings on the floors of real estate offices and Savannah's high-ceiling homes for Americans riveted by access to the oil-based, Cuban portraits. The pieces flew from my hands and the next couple of trips to Havana led me to the homes of various artists in search of more marketable items.

Alejandro, Luis, and I climbed dusty, beaten stairs in Old Havana to meet an artist living in a cubed apartment nearly wall-papered in lithographs and sculptures. We drove to the suburbs to view enormous, detailed countrysides by the prolific land-

Melanie and Luis in Alejandro Montesino's art studio (*courtesy of Melanie Simón*).

scape artist, Ernesto Estévez, and spent time with him and his extended family, who to the contrary, had a large, modern home.

Further sales allowed me to eventually set up a couple of shows in Savannah and interest was high. But perhaps more than just needed funds, the art gave us something positive to focus on until Luis's visa papers were approved and processed, whenever that was to happen.

And then, one afternoon in early January 2004, in one of my twice daily ritual calls to the US Visa hotline number, with the phone loosely holding on to the outer edges of my ear, I got a surprise: US immigration had approved our case. The phone went down, and I jumped and threw my arms around one of the girls at work. I swayed with her side to side, in crying, broken fits of laughter.

"What is it, Mel? What is it?"

I didn't say a word, locked on to her, and eventually, she cried and laughed, too, absorbing my joy for what it was.

After work, I raced home to call Luis, who was out and unreachable, and then Walter. Carrying on, over the moon, I was in midsentence when a powerful wave passed under my nose. It could have knocked me over. I froze, my eyes watered. It was my mother's scent—that distinct combination that belongs only to your mother.

I said to Walter, flatly: "Mom was just here."

He didn't say anything back. Maybe he thought I was crazy. I thought I was crazy. I found myself sniffing around the kitchen, desperate to understand. It had to have been an apparition or my imagination. But I knew, with all in me, that it wasn't.

Alone in the house, I was absolutely terrified, confused. I excused myself from the phone and went upstairs and sobbed. I came back down minutes later and sat at the kitchen table again.

A test of sanity, perhaps. Boom, in moments it happened again. Her scent, as vibrant as if she had been standing directly in front of me, whooshed under my nose again. I breathed in hard jerks, fighting to hold it because that time I knew my instincts were correct—my mother had just visited me. Yet she was gone just as quickly as she came.

I could only assume that she let me know that she was with me on that very big day, the one in which I knew that I had a real, tangible future with Luis.

I didn't tell another soul for ages and I never brought it up with Walter again. At times I wrestled with what had happened and questioned its validity. I wondered if my senses had simply conjured up her memory in a quest to make me feel even better on that day, though I wasn't consciously looking for her. But then again, maybe I was.

Yet, the same experience happened again and again, sporadically, over the next few years. Deep down I've always known it's her, not just a fluke of the mind. And while her brief appearances, which typically come at mundane and downright boring moments in my life—cleaning my house or watching a movie—used to upset me, I now appreciate them greatly. Her presence in this different form doesn't scare me anymore. I take her as she is and very much cherish her being near me. I do sink a bit and can't help but miss her, but I will always welcome those fleeting moments.

They are a great gift from her. My gift back to her is acceptance.

Chapter 47

Nooks, Crannies, and Saying *Adios*

L uis could have left Cuba the day after he got his visa from the US. He only needed a marked white slip on his end, simple enough to obtain. But he was nervous. He knew that he wasn't going to see to his family for a very long time—it could be years—as he waited for permanent resident status in the US. Policy here typically does not allow a resident-in-waiting to travel abroad.

By this time I had moved into the back apartment of my aunt and uncle's home, as they had so generously offered the space to us, rent free for one year, as a wedding gift.

I stood at the bedroom closet, the wooden door half-open, and pushed my hangers, clothes, and shoes to the right side of the narrow space. The left was open for Luis, and I stared at the emptiness for a good couple of minutes. What would he have with him when he arrived? And it was then, for the first time, that I allowed myself to think forward. I wondered what in the world he was going to do here. I couldn't imagine. He couldn't speak English and I didn't know where Spanish and Italian could take him in my Southern city.

In Havana, Luis set his mom up at home, hurricane prepping the windows and fixing nooks and crannies so that nothing was left undone. He tucked money into a cabinet she kept under lock and key. Then, one by one, he went to say good-bye to friends. Soon after he and his mom drove twelve hours into the deep countryside of Cuba where she had grown up and his grandfather, aunts, uncles, and loads of cousins still live today. With no running water and no electricity, he spent the next two months living simply.

Luis worked the farm with his family every day, just as he had done many summers since he was a kid. Though, this time, as he pulled the tough, rooted yucca from the ground, he tried to imagine life in the United States. His thoughts mimicked mine. What would he do? Would everything be different? Though his biggest curiosity surrounded me. Would our marriage be what he thought, and what would he do if it wasn't? And my family? If they were nutty, he was screwed.

Chapter 48

Miami-Bound

On Monday, March 8, 2004, more than three years after we first met, Luis hopped a plane in Havana, bound for Miami. Barren landscapes shaped the view below, but as he crossed to the Florida coastline rows of houses appeared in cookie-cutter form.

Luis passed through immigration without much difficulty and was directed to shuttles outside. After a short wait he boarded one for Sofitel Hotel, where I had made a reservation. He arrived before I did and opened the window of our room, watching the string of planes land one behind the other.

"*Y ahora?*"

What now? he thought.

When all you've done is work toward a goal, which is to have a life together, where do you put all of that energy once you've crossed the line? Especially once you get there and in place of celebration for finishing a race well done, all you hear is the pop of a gun, signaling the real race that's about to start.

Luis put his forehead on the window.

This is insane.

The train was accelerating at 150 miles per hour, and he was going to be OK if he jumped on it. But how?

The world's been moving, but I was stuck in the same place.

The elevator ride to the ninth floor of the hotel was the longest of my life. I knocked on the door and don't think I took a breath until Luis opened it. It was so unreal I didn't quite know what to do with myself.

Seeing him, I dropped my bag inside the door and gave him a long, tight hug around his neck. I must have sighed audibly. I pulled back, held his hands, and asked about his flight and his mom. It must have been wrenching for her to watch him go.

It didn't take long before we moved our conversation to the restaurant downstairs with two steaks and a bottle of red. Both nervous, excited, and without any road map for what was in front of us, we talked about where we started. It was mind-blowing to think about that first ride in his Cocotaxi where he pointed out El Morro, the very place we would later marry.

Afterword

The next day Luis and I pulled my green Honda Civic to the curb in front of my aunt and uncle's red brick home on the calm Savannah street. We grabbed his bags and walked around the side of the house and up one level to our one-bedroom apartment.

It was so quiet, he said. So quiet.

Within an hour, my father, who was on his way back home to Vidalia from North Carolina, drove an hour and a half out of the way to meet his new son-in-law. He appeared in our living room, just opposite Luis and though they were standing still, the crush of curiosity and energy bounced between them like a real, physical ball. It was intense. My dad's deep blue eyes brightened and grew in size, like I've never seen them, and reached for something familiar in Luis.

I translated gentle and polite comments between the two most important men in my life, hoping the conversation would stay light. It did. Before my dad left, he handed Luis a business card.

"You can get in touch anytime for anything," he told Luis.

But in Cuba there are hugs among family members and the business card felt cold. Luis told me later that he was offended. I explained that this was my dad's way of welcoming him and the gesture was well intended. This would be the first of many cultural misunderstandings.

Following, every Monday night Luis and I joined my father and grandmother for dinner, which Luis adored. My grandmother's dementia had already set in and she flirted with Luis showing the innocence of a little girl, telling him weekly how handsome he was.

In his own repetition, my dad asked the same three questions every meal: Do you speak English yet? To which Luis replied with a good laugh, "No, I've only been here a few days."

Have you found any work? "I'm looking. The problem is the language."

Finally, he wanted to know how Luis liked it here and if he was getting comfortable.

Luis struggled with his new cultural settings and missed his family desperately, but he always said yes.

After some time, we settled at our table at the Monday night restaurant, and before my father could say a word, Luis asked me to translate: "I still don't speak English, I haven't found work, but yes, I do like Savannah," and my dad almost fell out of his chair in a howl of laughter. They had grown to understand each other, on instinct, just as Luis and I had before our language gap closed.

We told him that Luis had picked up some work with my cousin finishing the exterior of a house, which led to questions about Luis's ability to do that sort of thing. I married MacGyver, I joked, and Dad offered to help Luis with a project if he found one. Luis left so excited he nearly ran circles back to the car. Within six weeks we had closed on a fixer-upper in a neighborhood close to the one in which we were living.

So began a string of DIY house flips and that same year Luis also started a small landscape company, buying the framework of an existing one with thirteen clients in Savannah. Today, more than ten years later, Simón Landscape has expanded to other communities in Georgia, as well as South Carolina.

We had our first child, Marcos, in 2007, just about the time I began transcribing detailed journals I had kept in New York and Cuba. Those formed the base of this book, which I drafted over the course of seven or eight years in the wee hours of the morning and thirty-minute lunch breaks. And as much as I love New York, moving back there never seemed like a smart choice. I probably could have settled back into city life, but once Luis moved to the US, Savannah seemed like the better choice, with both my family and job opportunities around.

Luisito moved from Guatemala to Houston with his mother and then with us in 2012, the same summer we had their little sister, Ana Luz. My dad and Luis talk about four times a day—in English—and my dad's nickname for Luis is Hombre. Not only is it one of the few words he knows in Spanish, but it comes from one of his Western flicks he watches religiously. The moniker is used for the good, tough guys who get things done. They have become incredibly close.

Luis became a US citizen in August 2014, and we are currently working on a visa for his mom to move here.